My Garden is your Garden

My Garden is your Garden

Patrick Daniell

Foreword by
The Rt Rev and the Rt Hon Lord Coggan
of Canterbury and Sissinghurst, PC, DD.

Illustrations by Pat Brockway
Garden plan by James Mulhall

Felix Publications

Published by Felix Publications,
Abbey Cottage,
Itchen Abbas,
Winchester,
Hampshire,
SO21 1BN.

Copyright © Patrick Daniell 2000.

All rights reserved.

ISBN 0 9537990 0 X.

No part of this book may be reproduced by any means, nor transmitted, nor translated into a machine language, without the written permission of the publisher.

A CIP catalogue for this book is available from the British Library.

Co-ordinated by Prospero Books, Chichester.

All colour plates except Numbers 3 and 4 were taken at Abbey Cottage.
Plates 3, 4, 6 - 18, 20 and 21 © Patrick Daniell.
Plate 5 © Michael Forrester.
Plate 19 © Peter McHoy.

Cover photograph:
The entrance to the walled garden at Abbey Cottage, Itchen Abbas.

Printed and bound in Great Britain.

Although every attempt has been made to trace the present copyright holders, we apologise in advance for any unintentional omission or neglect and will be pleased to insert appropriate acknowledgement to companies or individuals in any subsequent edition of this publication.

To my parents

Acknowledgements

I am very grateful to my sister and brother for their encouragement to write this book, and for their professional advice and support. I am delighted that they have involved their families in the thoughts and ideas we shared. Friends and visitors have also given me invaluable support and encouragement. I particularly appreciate Donald Coggan agreeing to write the foreword and thank him most sincerely. Amongst many other friends Pat Brockway deserves special mention for her detailed illustrations; and James Mulhall for the painstaking trouble and skill he devoted to his garden plan. Juliet Bloss, Carola Stuart, and Barbara Grunwell, with her team at Prospero Books, all deserve special thanks for their editorial and production work; and Alan Waters for his practical advice. I am grateful to both Michael Forrester and Peter McHoy who kindly gave permission for the use of their photographs.

I would like to thank:
The Society of Authors, as the literary representative of the Estate of AE Housman, for their permission to quote from his poem *A Shropshire Lad*.
AP Watt Ltd, on behalf of The National Trust for Places of Historic Interest or Natural Beauty, for their permission to quote from Rudyard Kipling's poem *The Glory of the Garden*.

Contents

Colour Plates			i
To Nature			ii
Foreword			iv
Introduction			15
Chapter 1	Design	- time for thought	17
Chapter 2	The Cottage	- a gardener's dwelling	26
Chapter 3	The Garden	- the heart of the matter	30
Chapter 4	My Plan	- the shape of things to come	34
Chapter 5	Construction	- hard labour	39
Chapter 6	Hedges and Trees	- the bones	49
Chapter 7	Borders	- flower power	63
Chapter 8	Grass	- green peace	78
Chapter 9	The Pond	- a Golden Section	83
Chapter 10	Fruit and Veg	- produce	87
Chapter 11	"Doing Gardening"	- practicalities	94
Chapter 12	Going Public	- added value	107
Afterword			115
Appendix	Some design principles		117
Bibliography			121
Index			123

Colour Plates

Plate 1   Aerial photograph - 1976
2   Aerial photograph - 1995
3   Jebel Akhdar, Northern Oman
4   Desert, Southern Oman
5   The garden - 1982
6   The garden - 1995
7   The view from the terrace
8   *Pyrus nivalis*
9   The pond garden
10   *Alchemilla mollis* (Ladies Mantle) and *Stipa gigantica*
11   Hebe
12   The allée
13   The meadow in spring
14   *Prunus sargentii*
15   *Juniperus chinensis* 'Aurea'
16   *Rosa* 'Parkdirektor Riggers'
17   *Clematis rehderiana and C. armandii*
18   Autumn colour
19   *Rosa* 'Phyllis Bide'
20   The box seat *Buxus sempervirens*
21   Shrub roses

To Nature

It may indeed be fantasy when I
Essay to draw from all created things
Deep, heartfelt, inward joy that closely clings;
And trace in leaves and flowers that round me lie
Lessons of love and earnest piety.
So let it be; and if the wide world rings
In mock of this belief, to me it brings
Nor fear, nor grief, nor vain perplexity.
So will I build my altar in the fields,
And the blue sky my fretted dome shall be,
And the sweet fragrance that the wild flower yields
Shall be the incense I will yield to Thee,
Thee only God! and Thou shall not despise
Even me, the priest of this poor sacrifice.

Samuel Taylor Coleridge
1772 – 1834

Foreword

My Garden is your Garden is a sheer delight, and I count myself highly privileged to contribute a foreword to it. It is the story of a realisation of a dream by the author during his army service in Arabia realised by hard work and loving care.

No detail is too small for his attention: look at the illustrations, especially the bus shelter, transported from the road outside to the garden.

The outline of the colour plan is made into a postcard and can become a bookmark with every book sold.

The book, like the colour plan of the garden itself, is meant to lure the reader on.

Let yourself be lured!

Good reading!

Donald Coggan.

Winchester.
23rd February 2000.

'Digging for victory'
The author with his grandfather and sister, Camberley 1942.

Introduction

"Tell me, how did you make this garden? What inspired you?"

"That's worth a book" I replied while I gathered my thoughts and guided my visitor.

"So why not start writing? And be sure to start at the beginning."

Making my garden has been sustaining work and a continuing pleasure that now includes this challenge to write. My book will become another part of the garden and just as I already share it with visitors, I shall share it more widely through writing. Some people say my garden is inspiring, others that it is extraordinary, and many say it gives great enjoyment. For me there is even more to it than that.

I recall the garden I knew as a child; it was just half an acre, but seemed much larger. The lawn was surrounded by rhododendrons and hollies; fuchsias, michaelmas daisies and hydrangeas flourished in borders edged with low box hedges, and a broken water pump with a long handle stood in one corner: in its chamber a robin built her nest. This garden at Brackenhurst, the cottage where we lived, belonged to the Kingsclear estate at Camberley in Surrey. My sister and I had the freedom to explore the estate and its walled kitchen garden where we investigated every corner. In the potting sheds and boiler houses we discovered and created mysteries, and in the glasshouses we admired the colourful carnations. We were each given our own small garden and grandfather encouraged us in our efforts. In return we helped him "Dig for Victory" in his allotment, and pulled on ropes attached to his lawn mower while he cut the grass. That was my childhood gardening.

At my first school I shared a small rectangular plot with another boy and grew annuals in lines like soldiers on parade - marigolds, asters, cosmos and larkspur were favourites. We tended our garden diligently and entered competitions that I hated not winning. At my second school I remember being allocated to do "land work" on a dismal piece of land known as

My Garden is your Garden

College Farm where we scavenged for potatoes - "spud bashing". I soon forgot that bleak experience when I worked for a nursery in Camberley where I gained confidence, and planted gardens that I revisit happily. Subsequently, during my career as a soldier I enjoyed a wonderful variety of gardens at home, in Kenya, Korea and Oman.

I found Abbey Cottage and its walled garden late in the summer of 1975. My feelings matched those of an unknown author who wrote: "I have never had any other desire so strong, and so like to covetousness, as that which I have had always: that I might be master of at least a small house and a large garden with very moderate conveniences joined to them, and there dedicate the remainder of my life to culture of them and study of nature". At Itchen Abbas near Winchester I had found the place to make my own.

This, then, is the story of my garden.

Abbey Cottage,
Itchen Abbas,
Winchester.

1st January 2000

Chapter 1

Design - time for thought

The garden at Abbey Cottage had been the kitchen garden for the former rectory at Itchen Abbas and at first sight I sensed the charm it embodied - a legacy of two hundred and fifty years' toil and care. The garden seemed to have a soul. Pevsner, in his book *The Buildings of England*, describes the rectory (now Abbey House) as one of Hampshire's finest 17th century classical houses. Although the rector's gardener may not have lived in a fine classical house, his cottage is a classic gardener's cottage built into the walls of a kitchen garden. I soon appreciated the potential for creating a new garden within these walls and immediate surroundings. Friends said they would be happy with just the area in front of the cottage; others commented on the situation, and the surveyor's report in 1976 might have deterred a more experienced gardener, but my instincts fired me with enthusiasm. For three years between 1976 and 1979 the walled garden behind the cottage enthralled me as I separated irises, paeonies and narcissi from the ground elder, took cuttings from the old box hedges, and enjoyed many varieties of apples.

I had no time at this stage to do major work in the garden, nor had I decided what to make of it, but I had an opportunity to capture a feel for the place until in 1979 I prepared for a very different opportunity in Arabia - to command the Sultan of Oman's Artillery. I visited Oman and the convenient flight from nearby Bournemouth, in one of the Sultan's aircraft, established an intimate link between that country and Abbey Cottage. During the summer of 1979 I revised my Arabic vocabulary in the shade of the apple trees in the garden, and also wrote a guide for the care of the plants. I gave this and the keys of the cottage to Cathy and Maurice Slapak, the owners of Abbey House who had agreed to take care of the place. I had regrets about leaving, but knowing I had a place of my own in England heartened me. In Oman I would make time to think about it - particularly about the garden.

I chose two gardening books to take to Oman in August 1979: Russell Page's *The Education of a Gardener* and Dame Sylvia Crowe's *Garden Design*. They seemed appropriate titles to study and with my photographs, survey and graph paper, were a valuable package beside my military papers. Little did I know how much I would enjoy studying the principles of garden design, gaining inspiration from gardens during holidays, and working my ideas into a plan which I ultimately drew full scale in the desert sands.

My work in Oman thrilled me and it became a privilege to be accepted in a foreign army. My service was continuing the assistance given over many years by the British Army to the Sultan's Armed Forces. Oman, the size of the United Kingdom, is strategically placed at the entrance to the Arabian Gulf and faces the Indian Ocean. The coastline is dramatic and inland the massive Jebel Akhdar or 'Green Mountain' dominates the northern interior and many square kilometres of desert (Plate 3). The indigenous population comprises 1.5 million people who are justly proud of their country, and gave me a warm welcome which reflected the wishes of a sultan of long ago; he hoped his country's association with England would "...continue until the end of time".

I found inspiration everywhere. In the high and remote mountain villages the tribesmen held their own against the rigorous climate, the terrain, and immemorial feuds. They were intensely independent and relied on what they could do for themselves and what their donkeys could carry up steep and rugged mountain tracks. They terraced slopes, grew olives and pomegranates, and dried fruit in the heat of the sun on the flat roofs of their houses. They cajoled eager spring water to irrigate the ground before it rushed in ancient conduits down the mountainside to the desert villages 3,000 metres below. In the intense light bright roses and hollyhocks added their colours to the predominantly green and brown shades. Every moment I spent on this mountain was inspirational. My garden featured regularly in my thoughts and I was enthused by knowing that like these villagers I had a place of my own, yet far away, to be nurtured and enjoyed. I wish the tribesmen who gave me hollyhock seed could know how they and their massive mountain influenced my garden.

The desert and its occasional villages were also inspiring. There I found the same water that had flowed in the mountain streams, but it ran more slowly. Villages named Bideeya, Minitrib and Yemen were based around their water supply which fulfilled many needs and which, before disappearing beneath the scorching desert, irrigated ancient walled gardens on a time sharing arrangement. In the centre of a village, as the shadow cast from a vertical post moved over marks on the ground, a 'sergeant major' arranged sluices which directed the water to irrigate specific gardens. In the heat of the day these walled gardens, and their seemingly neglected lemon trees, provided welcome shade and a peaceful situation similar to that in my own garden. Later in the cool of the evening I frequently enjoyed Omani friendship, often in 'companionable silence', sitting on the flat roof of a house, sometimes that of my driver Mohammed. Gazing through his date palms, I thought of the views framed by the trees surrounding the garden at Abbey Cottage.

Russell Page's and Dame Sylvia Crowe's books described principles and themes around which to work my inspirations. I would like to have met both authors because my thoughts and ideas accorded with theirs, and from them I gained sufficient confidence to enjoy this design phase of my garden creation. Russell Page emphasised the importance of having a feel for the site, and the ways of nature, before choosing plants appropriate for the soil and conditions. As a young man he worked for a time in partnership with Geoffrey Jellicoe and travelled in Arabia. He appreciated how Islamic life taught men to respect themselves and their neighbour, and how it helped them to find human dignity irrespective of rank and wealth. He also identified how life can be experienced other than from the European point of view - pertinent both for me as a soldier in a foreign land, and for anyone with or without a garden to make. My mind often dwelt on his definition of a characterless site: "a walled rectangle of sandy earth with not a tree in sight". He then described how there is always something to turn to for a starting point - he chose shade. He also included in his book instructive ideas about selecting and planting trees and shrubs - not least relating them to the type of soil in which they would flourish - and the use of flowers.

Dame Sylvia Crowe, who was for a time President of the Institute of Landscape Architects, complements Russell Page's book with her own on garden design, written for landscape architects. For me, an amateur, her book was a winner because she described in a straightforward way how the principles of design for large and significant gardens should also apply to smaller private gardens. Successful design, she emphasised, develops from a thorough assessment of the needs and characteristics of the site together with skilful incorporation of ideas, all contributing to an air of inevitability and a result which "...could be no other way". She described how the use of appropriate materials leads to unity and harmony and made me think about the flint and brickwork at home. Most importantly

Design - time for thought

Dame Sylvia outlined some design principles: unity; scale; time; space division; light and shade; texture; tone and colour and style.

I remembered these principles as I collected my thoughts and aspirations for the garden at Abbey Cottage. I wanted it to be original yet natural and in keeping with the surroundings, full of interest throughout the year, easy to maintain and united with the cottage. I owned an attractive and spacious site with unique charm and some old features. The sloping ground and position of the cottage at the lowest level presented problems, but these stimulated me to design the most significant elements of my garden - different levels and vistas. I realised also there is much to be said for looking up and through as opposed to down and onto plants and trees and my setting helped me make the most of these ideas. My story would be incomplete if I did not describe now how I followed three design principles (unity, scale and time) in my plan for the walled garden.

I would achieve unity by consistency of style and by joining the garden with the cottage and surroundings. To this end, having decided to extend the cottage eastwards into the walled garden, I would create vistas from the new doors and windows; these and a paved area would link the cottage with the garden. I would use flints and local bricks in retaining walls, and the same paving materials throughout the garden; there would, of course, be exceptions. My hedges would be mostly of yew, but if I chose other varieties - perhaps beech - I would plant sufficient to create unity.

I found the principle of scale helpful as I considered the size and dimensions of the terrace beyond the extension, the steps, the enclosures and the ornaments. Correct scale and proportion would contribute to the harmonious and peaceful atmosphere I wanted to achieve. The architectural ratio of the Golden Section[1] and a guide for the dimensions of steps[2] gave me rules with which to work.

---

1 A harmonic proportional ratio (a:b as b:a+c) thought to have originated in 6th Century BC. It is expressed as a ratio numerically as 1:1.618.

2 A useful guide is that twice the riser plus the tread should equal 0.43 metres.

As for the principle of time - will my design endure as the hedges, trees and shrubs flourish? My basic design is a classic one which should itself hold good, and in my vision I have accounted for growth and maturity. I hope that with essential care and maintenance my design which has a strong structure of hedges, walls and open space will remain a sound framework for the plants I grow.

The spaciousness of the desert helped me appreciate there is a limit to what the eye can absorb, and I had read about the enclosures or rooms in National Trust gardens. So on my paper I drew lines representing walls and hedges and combined the concepts of space and enclosure. The layout evolved as I adjusted the size and shape of the enclosures, made gaps in my imaginary hedges, and composed features of steps and slopes linking different levels. A paved area by the cottage, vistas, lawns and the open sky to the north would impart spaciousness. My initial design would reflect the formality, good order and singleness of purpose I know best - these are my style. The detail of intimate corners, their planting and ornament, would follow and supplement the framework.

Design - time for thought

During breaks from Oman I visited National Trust gardens at Hidcote, Sissinghurst, Tintinhull and Powis Castle, and gardens of a different style in Kashmir. In each I studied the detail of plants and recorded their names, characteristics and uses. I observed carefully the siting and construction of ornaments, edgings and steps, and filled my mind with ideas to complete my design. Later, while working in London, I often looked upwards and was inspired by many different roofs, finials and weather vanes.

At Hidcote I noticed the use of blue paint on woodwork throughout the garden, and decided to copy this with grey paintwork throughout my garden. I thought I could repeat the box seat in the white garden at Sissinghurst, and that a window in a yew hedge there might also find a place in my design. At Tintinhull the planting and list of plants within the different enclosures appealed to me for their quality and interest. At Powis Castle the use of ornament and the shape of the old hedges captured my imagination. My style is in keeping with these gardens, and the ideas from them that I have incorporated in my design are classic and enduring. It matters not, as Dame Sylvia Crowe explained, that my scale is smaller.

Discovering the garden at Jenkyn Place near Farnham excited me and that garden has inspired me more than any other. I sat by the pond and read the informative booklet that guided me round the garden in the way it was intended to be seen. I absorbed the garden's character, and sensed the care which Mr and Mrs Coke must have exercised in its creation sixty years ago. I told them I thought their garden rivalled Sissinghurst; "We think it's better," Mrs Coke replied. I was inspired by the formal layout, the informal planting, the selection of specimen trees, the choice and positioning of ornaments, and the way they had adapted the site and made many gardens within the whole: their garden was stylish and the quality impeccable. I learnt an enormous amount from Jenkyn Place and aspired to reproduce at Abbey Cottage some of what Mr and Mrs Coke had achieved. The beech allée in their garden was, in particular, something I hoped to include in mine. Ideas from Jenkyn Place and many other gardens helped me form my garden plans while serving in Oman.

My most memorable Omani gardening experience was when I drew my plan full scale in the desert sands (Plate 4). No-one else was in sight. My impressions in the desert will have disappeared long ago under windswept sands, but my thoughts at the time, and strong Omani influences, remain impressed on my mind. My English garden could never be in keeping with the harsh desert surroundings, but I readily imagined its formal structure with different levels and vistas, and even the water in the pond. I began to feel the ideas I had collected and adapted would result in a design which "...could be no other way". I vividly remember drawing those lines in the sand, and saying to myself "this is the garden I will make when I return home". That was the moment. My mind was taut and my vision clear. I am not so sure that "One is closer to God in a garden than anywhere else on earth" - maybe if one cannot be in the desert.

My outline design for the garden in front of the cottage and the walled garden were complete, although I would make slight alterations during construction. In due course I would make a gap in the northern boundary wall and extend the garden into the paddock. There, beyond the enclosure of the walled garden, I would develop less formal ideas. Initially I would restrict myself to a small area but I hoped, one day, to take in 3/4 acre (0.3 hectare) of the paddock.

I used the principles of unity, scale, and time as the basis for my design in the paddock. It is a fertile piece of grassland with good views across the Itchen valley. The garden I wanted there would include trees, an orchard, a vegetable plot, a nursery and work area, vistas, places to sit and a route to follow. Individual features linked by grass paths leading purposefully to their destination, and defining open spaces, would create the structure in the meadow.

The design, planning, construction and planting of my garden have taken nearly twenty years from the time I set out for Oman with an open mind and books to study, until now when I have set my boundary posts in concrete, and laid out the garden as I want. In Chapter 4 I will review that desert plan by taking my reader round the garden as I intend it should be seen, and imagining it as I hope it will become, but first let's discover the character of Abbey Cottage and its garden.

Chapter 2

The Cottage - a gardener's dwelling

Abbey Cottage is built into the southwest corner of the walled garden (Plate 1); it is thus united with the garden and part of this story. The building is a small delight at Itchen Abbas, a Hampshire village in the valley of the river Itchen - one of the world's finest chalk streams. The village takes its name from Saint Mary's Abbey, the old Nunnaminster in Winchester, and its Abbess, who owned land in the valley until the 16th century. There was never an abbey here, but when the Rectory was sold in 1926 it was renamed Abbey House, and the gardener's dwelling became Abbey Cottage.

The whitewashed brick and flint cottage was originally built on solid chalk without foundations, and had a thatched roof which inevitably caught fire. In 1840 William Bunney, the gardener for the rectory, lived in it with his wife Caroline and six children. He must have been a respected gardener because he won prizes and a medal[3] at The Horticultural Society of London's Winchester shows. His tiny cottage was extended to the north in 1953, and in 1982 I extended it eastward into the garden. Although the

---

[3] The medal is inscribed "The Horticultural Society of London at Winchester 1840, to Mr William Bunney, gardener to Mr William Campion Esq., Jnr, for the best exhibit during the year 1849".

physical connection with the walls is now broken, a paved area and new vistas from the cottage unite it with the walled garden - even more so than before.

Many people through the ages have enjoyed this beautiful area: there is evidence of Bronze Age camps, Saxon graves and Roman settlements. Pilgrims also made paths along the valley as they travelled between Winchester and Canterbury in the 13th century. Lord Grey of Falloden, Foreign Secretary at the time of the First World War, who saw "the lights going out all over Europe", knew the valley intimately for thirty years and owned a cottage by the river. In his book *The Charm of Birds* he describes the sights and sounds he enjoyed here during some of the most precious moments of his life. Lord Grey loved the river Itchen and its clear stream, as did Isaac Walton who fished the river at Winchester, and Charles Kingsley who was inspired by the river while he wrote sections of *The Water Babies*. My first impressions of the area reflected the atmosphere Lord Grey captured and described in his books.

My thoughts turned towards a house of my own in 1974 while I served in Northern Ireland. I wanted a place I could improve and develop, and where I could make a garden - over many years. During holidays I searched the Hampshire countryside, often accompanied by Aunt Stella who lived not far away. Her life was full of helpful kindness. She made friends with potential neighbours and quickly formed an opinion of every house we visited. Local estate agents said I was ten years too late but nevertheless flooded me with particulars of houses - one with "...garden mostly laid to concrete". Descriptions in many prospectuses seemed ideal until at first sight when the place appeared hopeless.

One evening my eye caught a prominent 'for sale' advertisement in *Country Life*. Beneath the description of Abbey House, and in much smaller print, was written "Further cottage and paddock also available". The London agents found it difficult to understand why anyone should be so keen to view the "further cottage" but I insisted and friends came with me. We enthused and I made an offer for the cottage but declined the paddock, which I could not afford. In due course, in December 1975, the owner accepted my offer and generously included the paddock; fortune was with me at this early stage. The surveyor's report was discouraging but I reckoned, very simply, the cottage would not fall down and its size and position were right. The place had great potential and I did not need too farsighted vision to picture the cottage as a jewel in my garden of joys.

I took possession in March 1976 and lived in the shed beside the cottage; it seemed best to allow a builder freedom to renovate the building, and if one is going to live rough it is easiest to do so in appropriate conditions. More importantly I had decided that nothing should take preference over my professional life as a soldier, and I did not want to be encumbered with the task of setting up house. I allowed myself just some weekends and holidays to attend to the cottage where my priority was to meet the building society's requirements.

Easter in 1976 was glorious and the cuckoo's arrival ever since has reminded me of it. I had never appreciated such birdsong and sensed being so close to nature. That holiday weekend, my first at the cottage, enabled me to leave my mark and as evidence I hung a door in place of the boards across the front entrance. My sister and brother-in-law planted potatoes in front of the cottage and, amongst other visitors, ten French

The Cottage - a gardener's dwelling

partridges walked in file along the garden wall as if they also owned the place.

A builder worked at the cottage during the spring of 1976 after which I was thrilled to spend a long summer leave there. I threw open the windows and doors which remained wide open for a month while the summer breezes penetrated the cottage. Two good soldiers, Bombardier Beckett and Gunner Koslowski, came to help; between us we removed trailer loads of debris and laid paths around the cottage. Our enthusiasm sustained us and after the building society approved our initial work I was able to continue as time and funds permitted.

I spent happy and constructive weekends and holidays at Abbey Cottage during the next two years and improved the building, but always stopped at lunchtime on Sundays to take stock and prepare for the week ahead. The surrounding undergrowth now cleared, the cottage stood with space around it for winter shrubs and plants to provide interest and scent close to the building. A flowering cherry, jasmine, mahonia, wintersweet, sarcococca, hellebores, aconites and snowdrops do just this. I have resisted planting climbers against the cottage; there is plenty of opportunity to grow them against the garden walls and the whitewashed brick and flint cottage walls are simple and attractive in their own right. Bearing in mind the welcome I wanted to give visitors, who would seldom arrive on foot and thus no longer use the sunken path from Rectory Lane to the front door, I planned a level area to the north of the cottage for a garage and ample parking.

As Abraham Cowley wrote in his poem *The Wish* in 1647: "May I a small house and a large garden have".

Let's go into the garden.

Chapter 3

The Garden - the heart of the matter

Since the brick and flint walls first enclosed this 1/2 acre (0.25 hectare) of Hampshire as a kitchen garden two hundred and fifty years ago, it can have changed little until I found it. My predecessors would recognise their garden from a photograph taken in 1971 when Mr Haines maintained a productive vegetable garden, just as he had done for more than twenty years. I often think of him and the other gardeners who have known the place as their own, exercised their varied skills here, and experienced their different hopes and fears. I think they would approve of their garden today; not necessarily for what I have made it, but because it is greatly cared for and their work is neither wasted nor forgotten.

The garden must have seemed large to those who cultivated it as a fruit and vegetable garden and dug it throughout by hand. But it does not seem large to me because the walls, trees on either side and neighbouring houses surround it and create a feeling of enclosure. To sense space I need only look up and the sky is the limit, or think of the adjoining paddock and beyond that of the open downs and farmland. I value these contrasting characteristics of enclosure and space.

In 1975 the building society's surveyor saw fit to comment on the garden as he surveyed the cottage. The dereliction and "pernicious ground elder" he so freely described in his report would have dismayed previous gardeners, but what he failed to describe, or maybe found it too difficult, was the garden's atmosphere created by an autumn harvest of colour and produce, the warmth of the micro-climate within the surrounding walls, and benign neglect.

The entrance from Rectory Lane is through a pair of wooden gates; twenty metres beyond these a wrought iron gate fills an opening in the garden wall. Here, at the principal entrance to the garden, the gate's craftsmanship, beauty and strength reflect the whole essence of the place, and throughout the day its framework catches one's eye. In the morning the framework is sometimes adorned with cobwebs illuminated like bright fibre optics. In the late afternoon when the colours in the garden intensify, the framework encloses the view as if looking through a keyhole. Finally in the evening, when the framework is silhouetted against the dark sky, it often dissects the rising moon above the eastern garden wall. Over the gate the canopy of an old Washington apple tree unites everything around this entrance but the tree needs a programme of careful attention if it is to remain such a feature. The tree's hollow trunk enables it to yield a little in strong winds and thus to have withstood the force of severe gales, the fiercest in 1987 when the tree was laden with fruit. I doubt this tree is as old as the three pear trees trained nearby against the western garden wall. They are fine specimens that regularly bear abundant crops. Behind the centre tree an old label is etched in copperplate: "Pear Beurre de Rance 1850 Dec - Mar". I think the label is original and I suppose there's a chance William Bunney wrote it. Would that lettering on today's labels lasted as long.

In 1976, standing at the entrance to the walled garden, the ground sloped gently upward (1:10) to the left and downward to the right. Ahead large unkempt apple trees flanked a narrow grass path. In three corners of the garden there were features; the fourth was empty. The cottage occupied the southwest corner. A large apple tree (Lady Henniker) and a spreading fig smothered rhubarb in the southeast corner. A broken water pump with a long handle, made by Mr Dibben of Southampton, stood in the northeast corner and beside it a ramshackle shed housed the vinehouse boiler. In this house were two venerable vines that must have produced grapes for many a rector's table. A cinder path edged with box hedges returned from the vinehouse past the empty northwest corner to the wrought iron gate and cottage. I have tried to perpetuate the garden's charm by making the most of all these features and the boundary walls that connect them.

The southern boundary wall is built entirely of flint with lime mortar but there was a gaping hole in it and sections were fragile. The eastern wall, another flint wall, is two metres high and capped with a course of tiles and semicircular bricks. Bounding the northern side of the garden is a three metre high brick wall built on deep foundations; in summer it's like a storage heater. At the top of this wall a line of hooks runs above a protruding course of slates. The hooks must have supported protection, held away from the wall by the slates, for the fruit growing there. The outlines of trained fan and espalier fruit trees are stencilled in the lichen on the wall which is also studded with generations of nails; some square headed, some with old cloth ties and others with lead tags. Between these nails five lines of wire, tensioned by raddiseurs, run the wall's full length. The western wall is built mostly of brick but there are flint sections; it is thirty centimetres thick and until 1953 continued beyond the wrought iron gate to become the front wall of the cottage. In this wall I found embedded miscellaneous pieces of metal, including the head of an old fork - it must have served some purpose. It is said that walls have ears and I would be intrigued to know all that these walls have heard.

The Garden - the heart of the matter

Although the garden lies in a frost pocket, its walls, and now its hedges, provide welcome protection particularly from damaging winds. The prevailing wind is from the southwest and over the years it and cold east winds have been more damaging than frost; except perhaps late frost in May. Despite frost's cruelty and the grief it causes, I find it easier to live with than wind, which can be relentless and destructive in any season.

I approached the re-creation of the garden and the renovation of the cottage with a long view, realising they would be significant tasks to exploit and enjoy. I wanted time to develop my ideas so that the ultimate results would reflect my thoughts and style. I set no timescale for completion but with hindsight it would have been twenty years.

Chapter 4

My Plan - the shape of things to come

In front of the cottage my plan is to have an uncluttered lawn and a generous parking area which will help create a feeling of space and tranquillity. The design here will be simple so as not to detract from the welcome I wish to make from the main features: the old apple and pear trees, a glimpse of the river, and a view through the wrought iron gate into the walled garden.

On entering the walled garden the hedged enclosures and varied levels will prevent the complete garden being seen in one view. However, obvious gaps in hedges should indicate there is yet more garden, encourage exploration and lead to surprise. I will allow the hedges to grow sufficiently high so as to conceal what is beyond them, but not so high as to be difficult to maintain. My plan unites the garden and the cottage but I want nothing to overshadow the latter, and will try to create the impression that the garden leads uphill away from the cottage as opposed to coming downhill towards it. The space created by the paved area to the east of the cottage will help achieve this.

The depth of the paved area (which I intend to call a terrace even though it is sunken) will be in scale with the cottage and an extension of it. For a grander house the ideal depth of adjoining paving would be the same as the height from ground level to the cornice. Abbey Cottage has no cornice, but using the height to the gutters should result in an appropriately sized terrace. In it I intend to make a rectangular rose border edged with box, and around it flint retaining walls, low enough to allow unimpeded views into the garden from a seat. The retaining wall on the north side must be higher and risks being daunting, so I shall build it with a batter and thus counter the effect of the ground sloping towards the cottage. I plan a broad and inviting flight of steps leading from the terrace up to a smaller paved area and a birdbath. Behind this I will build a low semicircular flint retaining wall; it will be concave - just a small detail to reinforce the impression that the garden leads away from the cottage and terrace. Here, the canopy of the old Bramley apple tree will unite everything under it: paving, steps, walls, birdbath and the western end of an allée. The allée, with a focal point at its furthest end, will create a new vista from the cottage. I intend to accentuate the allée's perspective by narrowing it slightly at the far end, and by careful alignment of the stripes of mown grass. The beech hedges on either side of the allée will be 2.5 metres high and shaped with a batter, thus creating a feeling of openness. At the end of the allée I will need to take account of the ground sloping upward to the left, and around an old apple tree (Lady Henniker) I will build another low semicircular flint wall. It will retain the surrounding earth at a distance of 2.5 metres from the base of the tree. The correct scale, proportion and detail in this corner of the garden will be important in order to achieve unity and harmony. Nearby I plan to place a seat within earshot of a fountain; from here the view towards the cottage and the herbaceous borders will be appreciated. Also, within sight of the seat, I shall have a window in the yew hedge, copying that at Sissinghurst, and allowing a view into the pond garden.

Herbaceous borders are labour intensive, mine all the more so for being far from water, tools and the potting shed. But I want them here for their interest and to turn this space into a separate colourful garden within sight of the cottage. The eye should then be taken across the lawn along the stripes of mown grass to a corner border. The entrance to the pond garden will soon become apparent and invite one to see more of what was glimpsed through the window in the hedge. Yew buttresses will flank the entrance to make it more noticeable from the wrought iron gate, and on either side I intend to plant the deep pink rose *Rosa* 'Beautiful Britain' which was the Rose of the Year in 1983. Backed by yew hedges the blooms should make a fiery spectacle, especially at dusk when their colour intensifies. The dimensions of the pond will be a Golden Section, and a fountain will be both the centrepiece in it and a focal point from the wrought iron gate. The fountain will also be a source of tumbling water, creating a tranquil sound to be heard throughout the garden.

Leaving the pond garden, and within a vista from the cottage (Plate 7), I plan a slope leading to the highest level in the walled garden. Steps with risers would stop the eye along this vista and be more difficult to maintain than a slope. So a wide grass incline edged with low flint walls will lead towards a grey gate in the corner of the garden. Here a water pump, a seat on a generous section of paving, a wide border and the vinehouse will all be features in front of the gate. The grass path will continue into the estate agent's "further paddock", or meadow as I prefer to call it. The meadow will be less formal than the walled garden - no more flint walls and paved areas.

In the meadow and visible through the grey gate a semicircular evergreen oak hedge will screen distant houses. At the centre of the semicircle I intend to place a sizeable sundial and nearby, at the end of a broad grass path leading to the northeast corner of the meadow, a bench seat under a tree. Every seat should serve a purpose and this one should encourage visitors to walk towards it and enjoy the young trees, the bulbs in spring and the view across the meadow and valley throughout the year. I want this view to include a feature which will attract visitors to a place from where they can enjoy the vista along the north side of the brick wall, and the plants growing in the shade against it. The vista will be towards the nursery, the work area and yet another bench seat where, as Rudyard Kipling wrote: "...along the thin red wall, you'll find the tool and potting sheds which are the heart of all".

I plan two lean-to sheds at the heart of my work area and nursery; they will be on both sides of the wall through which I will make a doorway. The view through this doorway, in either direction, will link the walled garden with the work area, the meadow and an orchard replacing one marked on an 1869 map. At the top of the orchard, the highest point in the garden, I plan to have a seat or a shelter to take advantage of the view across the valley. I want the complete meadow to seem like another enclosure in the garden, with the surrounding trees, the long wall and the grass paths uniting the whole.

Returning to the walled garden through the grey gate, the sound from the fountain, the vinehouse and a vista down the slope towards the cottage will be familiar, but I plan a new view westward. It will be framed by a yew hedge and the fine south-facing wall clothed with climbing plants; the eye will be carried across grass towards a prominent shrub in a corner. This view should be peaceful and uncluttered and I hope to resist all temptation to make another border in the grass. So that the plants growing against the south-facing wall may be appreciated and easily tended, they will be planted in a narrow border at its base.

Beyond the potting shed - with a view of the meadow through its doorway - I intend to retain the low box hedge and fill the border behind it with shrub roses. In this deep border I will lay stepping stones so as to avoid repeatedly damaging the soil structure when tending the roses. Finally, approaching the cottage, a golden juniper will mark the end of the yew hedge on the left; to the right are the wrought iron gate and the Washington apple tree. These features will form a group to be seen from several places in the garden and thus contribute to the unity of the design.

While developing my plan I have been mindful of every facility which will help meet my requirement to have a labour-saving garden - plenty of compost heaps, electricity and water points, and ease of access. But the enclosures, levels, borders, features and vistas are the main elements of the plan I will refer to during construction.

Visitors sometimes ask: "What do you think you brought to your garden from Oman?" An atmosphere of peace and space is my immediate reply, but with hindsight I would add patience. To my closest friends I would also add faith and the power of prayer.

Chapter 5

Construction - hard labour

I have enjoyed collecting garden equipment and materials wherever duty and holidays have taken me: a strong rake and a substantial watering can from a superstore in East Berlin are mementoes of just one adventure. Closer to home I collected railway sleepers and telegraph poles from the nearby section of the London to Winchester railway - the Watercress Line - while it was being demolished. I carried sleepers one at a time but manhandled sections of telegraph pole end over end - thankfully downhill. I was always on the lookout and discovered a local business which had recently cleared a nursery garden. A sturdy water cart with large iron wheels, made by Fred Smith of Basingstoke, a roller and other equipment found their new home at Abbey Cottage. I collected miscellaneous bricks, slates, tiles and assorted baulks of timber, which I knew would be useful one day, and I remember from where each came. When barracks in Aldershot and Winchester were being demolished and as opportunity and time allowed I removed useful pieces, and others scavenged from Whitehall skips, to Abbey Cottage. What a way to make a garden. Yes, but what a pleasure to make something from materials that would otherwise have been dumped. Other people considered these pieces junk; I valued them as building materials and stored them.

My duty in Oman ended in November 1981 when I returned home full of zeal for my garden. For a while I lived again in the garden shed and could not wait to begin work. I confirmed my plan and dug with a spade into the bank that came close to the rear of the cottage. Martin Roundell, a kind neighbour who has given me most of his gardening implements, saw me at work and wisely advised "...if I were you, I would get some good machinery". So I arranged with Mr Parfitt to bring his huge yellow digger to excavate the earth from around the cottage while I drove a dumper truck and removed his diggings. We started work on a bright February morning - 2nd February 1982.

Mr Parfitt was a tall, well-built man with a rugged, kindly face. He drove his digger into the walled garden through the gap which previous gardeners had blocked to keep out rabbits and Jack Frost. He manoeuvred his machine skilfully, inching the large bucket close to the cottage, and shifted tons of earth to make room for the extension and terrace. He matched the mirrors in his Cowley level with precision to plan a slight fall over the terrace and thereby ensure drainage away from the cottage. We removed many of the neglected apple trees, levelled areas for lawns, shaped banks, and took great care of the topsoil. For a time the garden looked like a desert and I wondered what I had undertaken, but there was no turning back (Plate 5). Mr Parfitt and I continued working together during a week of sunshine (how often the weather in the first week of February is good), after which my vision of the garden twelve years hence became more clearly focused (Plate 6). Twice that week a great friend, Michael Forrester, with his acute sense of knowing when support would be appreciated, visited and took photographs of some exciting days. Builders soon began their work and within three months completed the extension to the cottage with doors and windows opening into the garden.

I read that it takes seven years for a garden to begin to look mature - 1989 seemed a long time ahead. I would only have some weekends and holidays to spend at Abbey Cottage, but there was no need to hurry and I would be happy to take my time. Living and working in London during the week had benefits; to my great satisfaction I did not "live for the weekends" and fully enjoyed my work and other interests. Whenever my mind turned to Abbey Cottage it overflowed with details I noticed in the design of walls, paving and finials. I became intrigued with steps and at St Martin-in-the-Fields in Trafalgar Square I enjoyed proving the rule for the ideal proportion of risers and treads. I also enjoyed bicycling to work and passing bookshops where I knew I would be able to browse amongst the gardening titles in the evening. I visited Vincent Square and the Royal Horticultural Society shows where I learnt the names of plants, and used the Society's Lindley Library. What opportunities for learning and getting ideas, some of which I would develop and others discard, remembering the words of a fine commanding officer: "It's a good idea," he would say tellingly, "but we're not going to do it".

When my week's work in London finished I sensed a burning desire to get to my garden. Delays, whether in traffic or an overcrowded train, seemed interminable and I needed all my reserves of patience to survive the journey in an equable frame of mind. Opening the gates at Abbey Cottage was magical and in those first moments of a weekend or holiday the time ahead seemed endless. These were precious moments and similar to those Lord Grey described when he arrived at Itchen Abbas "...at some time between eight and nine o'clock, you step out of the train, and in a few minutes are amongst all the long-desired things. Every sense is alert and excited, every scent and everything seen or heard is noted with delight. You are grateful for the grass on which you walk, even for the soft country dust about your feet." At weekends I tackled project work on Saturdays, and on Sundays completed small but time consuming tasks until lunchtime, leaving the afternoon free for something different. Then I often walked to our church by the river for evensong before returning to London with flowers from the garden.

I made significant progress during holidays but also enjoyed refreshing breaks away amidst the hills and rivers of mid Wales. High in the Cambrian mountains between Tregaron and Rhayader, where brown grasses move like waves between rocky outcrops, I discovered the "desert of Wales" and while I absorbed the views to the east over the mountains I remembered that place of my own. My thoughts were often similar to those I enjoyed on the Jebel Akhdar, that massive mountain in Oman. In my garden at Abbey Cottage an acute Welshman might today identify a slate from his country, and a sharp-eyed Arab a stone from the edge of the Empty Quarter. Both these mementoes fit unobtrusively into my English garden - designed to be in keeping with the local surroundings.

I soon needed more flints than my scavenging in the garden provided so, like those before me who had built the garden walls with flints they collected from the fields, I took bags into the same fields and collected more. But results from repeated journeys did not match the pace of construction so I hired a truck. My diary for 26th August 1983 reads: "A very full day using a tipper truck to collect: three loads of flints from Itchen Down Farm; one load of sand - very full; two loads of ballast; two loads of sleepers and scaffolding; and two loads of manure. All very hard work but one day I will have a lovely garden". Tim, an experienced bricklayer who had a cheerful smile and a broad Hampshire accent, helped me build flint retaining walls and steps, and to rebuild the wall around the wrought iron gate. I enjoyed working as his apprentice, learning much more than just how to make a load of muck in the mixer. As Gertrude Jekyll described in *Home and Garden* "How well I got to know all the sounds. The chop and rush of the trowel taking up its load of mortar from the board, the dull slither as this moist mass was laid on a bed for the next brick in the course; the ringing music of the soft tempered blade cutting a well burnt brick, the muter tap of its shoulder settling into its place, aided by the down bearing pressure of the left hand; the sliding scrape of the tool taking up the overmuch mortar that squeezed out of the joint, and the neat slapping of it into the cross joint." Finally Tim and I rehung the wrought iron gate under its oak lintel and soldier course of bricks so that it now opens into the garden and makes a more welcoming entrance. Above the gate I have placed a stately unicorn - our family crest, and an image of its predecessors which featured in gardens in the Middle Ages (Plate 21).

By December 1983 I had completed the retaining walls and paving, rebuilt the vinehouse and laid water to it and electricity to the pond. Many bits and pieces which I had stored because "one day they are bound to be useful" had come into their own. There were others which, had I not discarded them only a short while before, I could also have used. The garden took shape as I moved miscellaneous piles of earth and filled the borders. Mr Norris levelled the lawns and Mr Radford and Mr Littlewood each in their turn lent a hand with manuring the borders. Throughout 1984 there were signs of growth and more progress as I planted hedges, trees and shrubs, although the growth of some was halted when I subsequently moved them. Since then David, Mac, Paul, Mike, Kevin, Dale, Edward, Charles and now James have in their turn each given me their help, and left their mark on the garden. I have enjoyed their assistance and hope they have good memories of their work here; between us we tackled some tough tasks but nothing defeated us.

Developments here must often have caused my neighbours to wonder, but I hope not too much. I have always been careful to consider their outlook and to give warning of work that might affect them. I hope none of my trees or structures have become too difficult to live with. On every side neighbours have been understanding and offered good friendship. At one stage Martin Roundell became interested in the neglected southeast corner of the meadow where I had my rubbish heap and where he wanted to extend his cottage. Our mutual solicitor met us and we agreed a price for the land - including the rubbish.

Tim returned with Sam, a carpenter, to slate the roof on the shed which had been my bedroom; I watched them carefully knowing that one day I would enjoy doing similar work. I began to study the detail of buildings resembling those I had in mind to make (including a hut on Romney Marsh, the design of which appealed to me) and which would soon became a satisfying part of construction. I learnt the names and purpose of different roofing timbers - rafters, purlins, trusses and plates - and hankered to incorporate them. I bought slate cutters that severed and chamfered slates as if they were butter, and I learnt the importance of matching the overlap of these slates to the pitch of the roof thus preventing water creeping between them. Then, with the point of a slater's hammer, I made countersunk holes in Welsh slates and through these hammered broad-headed nails into wooden roof battens.

In the vacant northeast corner of the garden I built one lean-to potting shed, made a doorway through the wall, and built a similar shed on the other side. Railway sleepers, telegraph poles, roofing timbers from Martin Roundell's cottage, and door locks and bolts from my parents' old garage all became part of the construction. I dismantled my own small wooden garage just before a violent storm blew down trees across Rectory Lane; they fell where the garage and a precious old car had been standing only days before. Ivor and Graham came to remove the trees, and built walls for a new garage. I followed them and slated the framework of rafters and trusses that formed the roof, and then clad the walls with panels from the old garage. These buildings show hallmarks of my amateur work, as do many elements of my garden construction, but they all contribute to the style which helps make the garden look my own. I now had appropriate space to store equipment in its rightful place and thus save valuable time by having what I needed readily to hand.

In one corner of the pond garden I wanted a shelter of a certain size. I noticed the design and detail of many shelters and formed a picture in my mind of something quite unaffordable. It can only have been Providence and my thoughts of shelters which encouraged me to repair the bus shelter at the bottom of Rectory Lane. It was an attractive old shelter, with a cedar shingle roof, but age and weather had taken their toll and vandals had recently overturned it. I enjoyed repairing the damage which took me some time, but in the end the shelter was in better shape. No sooner had I returned to the cottage than I heard hammering from the direction of the shelter and returned hastily to accost the vandal. I was astonished to find a man trying to dismantle the shelter, which he intended to replace with a new one he had brought on a trailer behind his car. He admitted having difficulty - which gave me wicked satisfaction - and said he would be taking the old shelter away to burn it. I offered to take it away for him and then and there lent him a careful hand. The shelter matched exactly that which I had in mind for the corner of the pond garden (Plate 9). It stands there today complete with a bus timetable and my story which concludes: "This shelter has protected many people in the past and I hope it may shelter many more, but please don't expect a bus."

I searched and found a statue to complete the vista from the cottage along the beech allée. Hebe - cupbearer to the gods - clothed with dignity and dutiful now stands serenely at the eastern end (Plate 11). How I enjoyed searching for her, and the fetching and carrying, and how true that has been of all my ornaments, but I was wary of collecting too many. Martin Roundell's wife, Louise, advised me early on "not to have too much that is not alive in your garden". I think she offered this advice in relation to a stone owl that took my fancy but was difficult to place. The owl flitted around the garden and she probably noticed it during several visits and thought I had more than one. Anyway it now roosts in a corner of the bus shelter - just as if it should never have roosted anywhere else. A sundial, a large plaque set against a wall, a flagpole, finials and a weather vane are other ornaments I have enjoyed considering, finding and installing.

I sited seats throughout the garden according to my plan and where there is a good view; they look permanent and are focal points. I prefer those I have repaired to those bought new - whatever their quality and cost. One hot day Tim and I, while building the terrace wall, sat on it at a convenient level and realising what a good place it would be for a seat immediately made one in the wall.

Amongst the many items I have been given is a handsome gate for the gap in the wall by the pump. The hinge is cleverly designed so that as the gate opens its axis moves from the vertical allowing the end furthest from the hinge to rise - a useful method of overcoming the effect of opening a gate against sloping ground.

I won a best-kept lawn competition and spent the prize on a large stone sundial, with a simple armillary sphere, which now stands at the centre of the semicircular evergreen oak hedge. I collected it easily from Kent, but moving it the final hundred metres was a struggle involving rollers, planks and plenty of muscle. Subsequently moving a large plaque across the meadow and fixing it against the wall, in the furthest corner, was another struggle which required ingenuity. The plaque is a handsome one picturing Hades transporting Persephone between Mount Olympus and the Underworld. Part of the legend is that Persephone was happy and scattered plants along the route. I have imitated her happiness and scattered daffodils myself in the border beneath her plaque.

Inspiration for a weather vane came to me during a meeting in London while I gazed out of a window towards Wren's domes and spires - some supporting golden weather vanes. The meeting lasted long enough for me to conceive a design; afterwards, as I walked though St John's Square in Clerkenwell, I noticed a metalsmith who sold me copper sheet that I needed for the motif. A talented artist, Lydia de Burgh, drew an outline of barnacle geese which often fly up and down the valley. I traced this onto the copper and cut around the geese which although fixed as my weathervane nevertheless 'fly' on the cottage roof and are totally in keeping with the surroundings.

Construction - hard labour

In 1990 I started construction in the meadow and hankered after using a mechanical digger. I hired a small self-drive machine and although I lacked Mr Parfitt's skill I mastered the controls and achieved quickly what would otherwise have taken weeks of hard work. For three warm autumn days in early October I dug trenches for hedges and water pipes, holes for trees, and prepared foundations for frames and a greenhouse. In my search for paving slabs to edge borders Providence was with me yet again. We went to Basingstoke and Winchester where streets were being pedestrianised and the contractors were only too glad to give away their unwanted slabs.

Another worthwhile construction has been a shelter near the top of the orchard. A seat would have sufficed but here was an opportunity to build something more substantial. My mind ran riot with ideas. Eventually I made a rectangular framework that I clad with feathered larch planks, and constructed a roof with larch rafters and cedar shingles fixed with bronze nails. A computer-programmed saw would have cut perfect angles at the end of each rafter which supported the hipped roof but, without that saw and after many measurements and pencil lines, I found cutting by eye produced the best results. In the shelter's large side openings secondary double-glazing panels, collected from Winchester's Recycling Centre, provide protection from winter weather. Wooden slats replace these panels in summer and allow breezes through the interior just as delicate window tracery serves the same purpose in Arabian buildings. The shelter's construction was a most satisfactory occupation and while working at it I enjoyed the view southward across the valley. I completed the shelter just before Christopher Corbally, one of the Pope's astronomers, visited and so it became the 'Observatory' and from it I watched the comet Hale Bop in February 1997.

Finally, my most recent construction has been an outside loo; the clank and clatter of its elderly Antelope cistern regularly joins the garden's other characteristic sounds.

I have enjoyed good health, invaluable assistance, and learnt an enormous amount during the fifteen years construction has taken. I have made many mistakes - borders and gaps too narrow, depressions in lawns, awkward corners and insufficient water points - to list just a few. The thrilling moments I had sensed on arrival home in the early days would be replaced as I became a resident rather than an absentee. Plants, wildlife and horticultural aspects, which until now had taken second place to design and construction, would be more in my mind as I began to feel - like a fish in water - entirely in my element.

"If you wish to be happy for ever and ever make a garden."[4]

So far so good.

---

[4] Ancient Chinese proverb.

Chapter 6

Hedges and Trees - the bones

In my desert plans I easily imagined tall and firm hedges but it was harder, in my garden, to accept that the young hedging plants would ever make a complete structure. The hedges, and the three large apple trees I saved, are fundamental elements of my design.

In 1976 the low box hedges *Buxus sempervirens* 'Suffruticosa' that edged the path between the cottage and the vinehouse were the only hedges in the garden. I wanted to retain them but they were unsuitably placed, so my brother took cuttings and I reluctantly removed all but the section of hedge which now surrounds a border of shrub roses. I have no regrets but I hope I will resist temptation to replace this remaining section of hedge which helps the garden retain its charm.

New hedges would meet my requirement for space division and enclosure, and would provide a background for plants, conceal retaining walls, and grow into garden features. Box, yew and beech would be classic and natural choices for the walled garden. I would use hornbeam, quickthorn, hazel and evergreen oak in the meadow.

I set these criteria for the hedges:
- each hedge should serve a purpose in my design.
- the rate of growth would be immaterial.
- in the walled garden the hedges should be formal.

and that I should:
- have easy access to the hedges.
- be able to cut most without using a ladder.
- have variety but avoid detracting from the unity hedges will create.

My brother's cuttings from the mother box hedge, planted at twenty centimetre intervals, make a low hedge around the rose border on the terrace; individual *Buxus sempervirens* 'Handsworthiness' and *B. sempervirens* 'Aureovariegata' conceal the ends of walls and define particular garden areas. I have successfully grown eight *B. sempervirens* 'Handsworthiness' to make a bench seat in the pond garden (Plate 20). It is a copy of the seat in the White Garden at Sissinghurst and an eye-catching horticultural feature. It takes the place of what might otherwise have been an ornament and meets Louise Roundell's exhortation not to have too much that's not alive in the garden. A knowledgeable and observant gardener, Lady Coggan, visited the garden and helpfully suggested this seat would look more comfortable with cushions; so I am growing cushions of box which I will trim and sink, in their pots, in holes in the wooden bench.

I have planted 100 metres of yew *Taxus baccata* hedging to divide the walled garden and create enclosures. In place of lines in desert sands, I dug deep trenches and forked in plenty of manure. Then, in September, I planted young hedging plants each with an equal amount (forty centimetres) of top and root growth, and kept them well watered for their first year. Subsequently, for two years, I fed them with 'blood fish and bone' and trimmed them carefully with secateurs - cutting out inward growing and crossing shoots and shortening other strong shoots to a point where new growth was breaking. I left one leader uncut on each plant until it reached fifteen centimetres below the hedge's ultimate height. These young plants, like most in my garden, took two years to settle and since then have grown steadily into firm hedges. Yew are greedy plants - hence their strong growth - but plants in my borders which are backed with yew do not seem malnourished and the hedges provide a superb fresh green background in summer. Yew knocks spots off its competitors and my advice to visitors concerning hedging is absolute: "by all means consider alternatives but I hope you choose yew". Yew is the queen of hedges and at Abbey Cottage *Taxus baccata* rules.

Beech *Fagus sylvatica* is a princess of hedges. There is only a brief period in April when it is bereft of foliage and looks sparse, but then it is exciting to watch the buds swell and burst as they release their tightly packed young leaves. What vitality! The first beech hedge I planted in 1977 was a double one and now stands as a wall three metres high between the garden and the western part of the meadow. In December 1983 I planted two lines of single beech hedging to create an allée similar, but on a smaller scale, to that at Jenkyn Place (Plate 12). The plants were young saplings from the backwoods of Aldershot and on planting I reduced their height by one third. I cut them every July and shape them with a batter, so they are wider at the base than the top; as a result they appear well anchored and the allée seems light and open. I admire beech leaves for their fresh green colour in spring, their deeper green in summer, and later their russet colour which brightens grey afternoons in November - sometimes described as the most dismal month of our year: "no sun, no moon, no morn, no noon - November".

A semicircular hedge of evergreen oak *Quercus ilex* is another princess of hedges; it surrounds the sundial in the meadow beyond the grey gate and is 2.5 metres tall. The need for a screen was obvious; that it should be a closely clipped hedge of evergreen oak was an idea inspired by an evergreen oak tree I noticed closely clipped in a Kentish garden. The plants have grown together well and their shiny foliage, although sometimes burnt by cold winds, is an attractive shade of dark green. The whole is an arresting feature - literally - causing visitors to check the sundial's time and to admire the meadow.

Hornbeam *Carpinus betulus* is a handsome prince of hedges, similar to beech but with heavier growth and more deeply ribbed leaves. One young hedge forms a boundary for the orchard and is in keeping with it - more so than beech would be. In spring I tie the hedge's long upright leaders horizontally to encourage fresh growth to break along their length and thus thicken the hedge.

Quickthorn *Prunus spinosa* is a rather rebellious prince of hedges; it requires much attention which its thorns impede, but it is tough, quick growing, and provides a sanctuary for nesting birds. I planted a quickthorn hedge along the boundary at the eastern end of the meadow and for several years cut it back by a third to encourage thick growth at the base; thereafter it soon grew to make a good hedge. I trim it as and when required but unfortunately this seems to be more often than not. I regret ivy has taken a hold and will soon smother the hedge and that will be a shame, but there it is, ivy is rampageous and its roots lie far beyond my reach.

The youngest hedge in the garden is a mixture of twenty or so miscellaneous hedging plants which were reserves in case of failures. These surplus plants have come into their own and are growing as a mixed hedge along the northern boundary in the meadow. For the present each variety gets individual attention but soon I will not discriminate. In royal parlance this hedge is a mistress but no less attractive for being so.

These hedges are rewarding me for the trouble I took in deciding their purpose, their planting and their subsequent care; together with the old apple trees they form the garden's framework.

The names of the apple trees in the garden reflected people and places connected with their introduction, and I am glad to have identified these before I reordered the garden. Laxton's Superb, Washington, American

Mother, Lady Henniker and Worcester Pearmain were some of the twenty or so apple trees planted here this century, but they had become overgrown and dominated the garden. I thought about retaining them but spared the axe for only three: Bramley, Lady Henniker and a Cox's Orange Pippin. These are anchors in my design and help retain more of the garden's charm and character.

Many native trees surround the cottage and I look upwards and outwards to enjoy them. Ash, beech and a line of Leyland cypress, which provide protection from northeast winds, break the northern skyline. To the east a solitary conifer in my neighbour's garden dominates mine but its stark effect is reduced by a copse of mature beech in the background. To the south there is a shapely sycamore and beside the river are poplars whose rustling leaves add to the garden's summer sounds. Further away across the valley alder, oak, beech and lime make a collection of native trees. To the west, in the grounds of Abbey House, are fine specimens of cedar, chestnut and walnut. Indigenous and noble trees thus surround this garden in which I have ample space to plant young specimens. Choosing trees for the garden, selecting them, and bringing them here has been memorable - each tree could tell a story. I set these criteria for the trees. They must:

- be suitable for the soil.
- in keeping with the surroundings.
- have special attributes.
- serve a purpose.

The majority of my trees have been bare rooted specimens and if I was starting again I would add this criterion to my list. Trees in containers are probably healthy enough, but they seem reluctant to spread their roots into soil to which they are not accustomed, so I would always choose bare rooted trees and plant them in their dormant season. I am prepared to enjoy and nurture young trees; other people will, I hope, enjoy them in their maturity.

Walks in the Hillier arboretum beyond Winchester and visits to other gardens gave me ideas - too many - and nursery catalogues and books provided more. I checked and cross-checked the shape, size, foliage and blossom of possible trees and made long lists, but my limit for the walled garden was just fifteen trees including two pairs and a trio.

In front of the cottage, near the entrance from Rectory Lane, an autumn cherry *Prunus subhirtella* 'Autumnalis' provides a cheerful sight westward and a welcome for visitors in winter. On the terrace *Sorbus vilmorinii*, a small tree, has pinnate foliage which provides some shade but does not take light from the cottage. This sorbus has grown into a sturdy tree with an attractive framework of branches and autumn foliage. It has everything to its credit - all the more so because although it is growing in a deep pocket of good soil, this is surrounded by chalky subsoil in which there can be little goodness.

A trio of junipers *Juniperus scopulorum* 'Skyrocket' at the edge of the terrace screen a neighbouring window. Their rate of growth has matched their name and they are well furnished with foliage despite growing in a shaded and draughty position. They take the minimum of light from both my neighbour's window and the terrace, and their evergreen foliage contrasts well with beech leaves and the flint wall.

A flowering crab *Malus tschonoskii* breaks the roofline of neighbouring Itchen Gate and conceals a chimney. This fastigiate tree meets my criteria because it is in keeping with the two nearby apple trees, it takes little light from the herbaceous borders, has delicate crab apple blossom and the colour of its autumn foliage lives up to its description - the bonfire tree.

The paperbark maple *Acer griseum* is near the top of my list of trees. The colour of its bark and foliage make it a very attractive small tree. There were many possible positions for it, but its size led me to plant it closer to the centre rather than the perimeter of the garden. It would, however, be lost on its own so I planted it in a corner made by the yew hedge surrounding the herbaceous borders; it will contribute useful height there and its brown flaking bark will always be of interest.

An ornamental pear *Pyrus nivalis* has grown to eight metres since 1984 and is an attractive round headed tree (Plate 8). The silver weeping pear *Pyrus salicifolia* originally tempted me but I wanted a larger tree to fill a corner and to be seen throughout the garden. The fresh green and grey foliage, closely followed by white blossom, ranks high amongst springtime attractions. When the freshness of the foliage fades to an olive colour the habit of this tree complements the large apple trees and contributes to unity within the garden. I have yet to find a purpose for the small rock hard fruit but that does not matter - the tree is one I recommend.

On the main lawn, with a background of yew, there was space for a pair of trees six metres apart; interest throughout the year would be a priority for trees in this prominent position. Magnolias caught my eye amidst the glory of spring but they seemed to fail the alkaline soil test until I discovered *Magnolia x loebneri* 'Merrill', two of which now flourish in the lawn (Plate 6). Against the yew background they are superb. In winter their framework of strong growth with furry buds is silhouetted, in spring the blossom looks whiter than white, and throughout the summer the green and brown foliage strengthens the garden's colours.

A golden juniper, *Juniperus chinensis* 'Aurea', was the first tree I planted in the garden (Plate 15). I saw a fine specimen growing in the arboretum at Castlewellan in Northern Ireland. My mother's family (Annesley) planted this arboretum at the end of the 19th century and I enjoyed exploring it. Friends took a cutting and several years later brought it to Abbey Cottage; it was not difficult to adjust my criteria for such a special tree. It is a focal point and landmark at the end of a yew hedge with lavender *Lavandula angustifolia* at its base. This conifer also incorporates my mother's family with the garden.

A fastigiate Irish yew *Taxus baccata* 'Fastigiata' and a pair of Irish junipers *Juniperus communis* 'Hibernica' might be thought out of place in a Hampshire garden, but they are excellent ornamental trees. The yew was a rogue amongst a batch of hedging yew but now it stands strong and straight as a landmark and in contrast with the horizontal slats of the seat near the pump. It casts little shade and by banding it with wire I prevent it becoming lax. Beside this yew the delicate framework of June Berry *Amelanchier lamarkii* shows against the sky above the eastern boundary wall. In April this tree's fragile white flowers are a gentle sight when young bronze leaves accompany them; in autumn these leaves colour brilliantly. It is not a sufficiently significant tree to be a single specimen but beside the yew and a rose *Rosa rubrifolia* it earns its keep. Nearby, in the pond garden, the two Irish junipers *Juniperus communis* 'Hibernica' stand like sentinels, their sea-green foliage in delicate contrast with the darker green yew hedge. The vertical lines of these trees complement the upright corner posts of the bus shelter.

It is said that "man plants trees for posterity"; on reflection I hope whoever planted the trees I enjoy now as mature specimens enjoyed them as young trees and to the same degree as I enjoy mine. Choosing, planting, and caring for every tree has given me an affinity with them - to the extent that as Coleridge wrote: "Friendship is a sheltering tree".

Each tree in the meadow has special characteristics and because several are fastigiate I am able to accommodate more than I could otherwise. There have been failures, but not many; lack of water, wind, frost and rabbits have taken their toll of a mulberry *Morus nigra*, a *Liquidambar stryaciflua*, three *Koelreuteria paniculata*, and a sorbus with huge leaves *Sorbus thibetica* 'John Mitchell' which blew down in a gale. I enjoy each of the trees I have planted for varied reasons and during different seasons so it seems best to describe my top twenty alphabetically:

Aesculus indica - Indian horse chestnut. This will become a very large tree, perhaps twenty metres high and is a tree for the future. It has attractive smooth grey bark and large shiny sticky buds in winter. Pink flowers develop from panicles that open in late June or July - a good time to have a tree in bloom.

Aesculus parviflora. This is truly a shrub, because it forms a head of branches near ground level as opposed to a tree, which develops its branch system on a trunk. I have planted it as part of my tree collection to meet the needs of a particular position in front of a neighbour's house, the view from which I do not wish to obscure. It will grow to a height of 2.5 metres and develop a similar spread. It should flower even later than a horse chestnut and have white flowers with red anthers on slender panicles.

Betula pendula 'Dalecarlica' - Swedish birch. This tree will grow tall and slender with drooping branches and deeply incised leaves. No garden would be complete without silver birch, sometimes called "the lady of the woods" - a description which in itself is good reason for its inclusion in my collection.

Betula utilis var. *jacquemontii* - Himalayan birch. Beautiful white peeling bark is the outstanding characteristic of this medium-sized tree. The upright growth of a group of five makes an attractive framework against evergreen Leyland cypress. My group originally comprised just three trees which seemed rather few and an additional two have made a significant difference.

Catalpa bignionoides 'Aurea' - Indian bean. This is a decorative tree with bold heart-shaped golden leaves that are, sadly, vulnerable to being torn by the wind. The flowers should increase as the tree matures, they are white with yellow and purple markings and bloom in July and August; long thin beans follow them. Maybe it's a tree not altogether in keeping with the surroundings but its foliage and late flowering justify its place in my collection.

Cedrus deodara 'Aurea' - Golden deodar. I first noticed this tree in a Welsh garden and found my specimen at the Westonbirt arboretum in Gloucestershire. It will become a beautiful large conical tree with golden yellow foliage in spring, turning green in summer.

Cladrastis sinensis - Chinese yellow wood. This little-known tree belongs to my collection but only in my mind's eye - at present. It is a distinctive medium-sized tree, which flowers in July. I saw it at Jenkyn Place where

Mrs Coke gave it a high rating. I have failed to find it for sale which makes me all the more determined to have it growing here either from seed or by grafting it onto *Cladrastis lutea*. What interest I have enjoyed searching for this tree which must, for now, remain twenty first on my list.

Crataegus prunifolia. This is proving an excellent compact tree that will eventually grow medium-sized with a round head. In winter its purple brown twigs are striking; in spring dark glossy leaves break from these twigs and then in autumn turn bronze; together with a mass of red fruit, they set the tree ablaze.

Fagus sylvatica var. *heterophylla* 'Asplenifolia' - Fern leafed beech. Any beech is a noble tree and this is a special variety amongst many others. It will make a medium to large tree of rather upright growth. Fernlike leaves, dissimilar to those of any other beech, are the tree's most interesting characteristic. It is an unusual and attractive tree in keeping with the surroundings.

Fagus sylvatica 'Purple Fountain'. I played as a child under the canopy of a weeping copper beech and much wanted to include a specimen in my collection; it will fill a space near the Golden Catalpa and the two will look good together.

Fraxinus excelsior 'Jaspidea' - Common ash. A vigorous clone that will make a medium-sized tree with golden yellow young shoots and foliage. I am growing it to screen an electricity pylon which it is doing quickly and effectively.

Ginkgo biloba - Maidenhair tree. When you cannot find this tree listed in the general section of a catalogue then turn to conifers. It is an exceptionally interesting medium-sized ornamental tree and the sole survivor of a prehistoric family. Its deciduous fan-shaped foliage becomes pale golden yellow in autumn and makes a warm-looking carpet at leaf fall when sometimes it sheds all its leaves overnight.

Ilex aquifolium 'Argentea Marginata Pendula' - Perry's silver weeping holly. Another tree from Westonbirt where its growth of strong weeping branches caught my eye. It will become a graceful compact tree which should bear many berries, but mine like most hollies is slow to grow - one day it will be a shapely tree.

Juglans regia - Common walnut. The prospect of having my own walnuts encouraged me to include this tree. It is rather a slow growing medium to large-sized tree that will eventually become a distinctive shape and a beacon for rooks who enjoy collecting walnuts. This tree and the catalpa are vulnerable to late frosts and sensibly delay breaking into leaf - another of nature's wonders.

Magnolia grandiflora 'Exmouth'. It is touch and go whether I will grow this magnificent tree successfully in the meadow where its large evergreen leaves are so easily burnt by frost and cold winds. But it's worth trying just for the large pale yellow lemon-scented flowers that should be in evidence throughout the summer. These flowers are often produced at an early age - an added and glorious bonus.

Ostrya carpinifolia - Hop hornbeam. I hope this will grow into a medium-sized tree with all the good characteristics of its related hornbeam - shapely growth, ribbed and toothed foliage and autumn colour. In addition long drooping catkins should hang like hops from its branches in spring. I saw a similar tree growing in Tuscany and enjoyed researching its merits.

Prunus 'Accolade'. This is a very early flowering cherry that will become a small tree with spreading branches and strong pink semi-double flowers. It is a cross between that invaluable early flowering cherry *Prunus subhirtella* and *Prunus sargentii*.

Prunus avium 'Plena' - Wild cherry - double gean. A. E. Housman wrote about this beautiful woodland tree in his poem *A Shropshire Lad* "Loveliest of trees, the cherry now is hung with bloom along the bough, and stands about the woodland ride wearing white for Eastertide". From this tree most of our sweet cherries are derived. It will grow to a medium size and bear heavy clusters of double pure white cup-shaped flowers. It never flowers for long enough.

Prunus sargentii. A tree which is regularly top of my list for its repeated contribution to the garden. It is a small tree with bronze red young foliage, single very delicate pale pink flowers, and deep crimson foliage in autumn. I am sad to see this energetic tree lose its foliage in November but by then it deserves a rest (Plate 14).

Tetradium danielli. This tree has yet to prove its worth but I had to include it in my collection. It was introduced from Korea by a naval surgeon captain, William Daniell (1817-1865). Its merits are that it is a fast growing small to medium-sized tree which flowers in late summer. There must be some disadvantage because otherwise it would be better known, but I grow it in hope, expectation and because of the name.

Tilia henryana - Lime or linden. Another tree from Jenkyn Place and fast proving its worth. Described as a very rare medium-sized tree, mine is growing well and should flower in the autumn. Its handsome serrated leaves are coloured deep sea-green edged with carmine. These invite attention and study; they are yet another "Glory of the Garden".

Two more trees in the meadow merit special mention even if only for the record. I planted one, a copper beech, in 1977 to commemorate HM the Queen's Silver Jubilee; the other, an English oak, grows from an acorn taken from a tree which stood in the grounds of Winchester College until the October hurricane in 1987 felled it.

This collection of trees is an interest and an investment paying a good dividend. I have learnt from my mistakes and might, with greater confidence, have been even more careful in selecting each tree and rejecting any without a good straight trunk and balanced top growth. I have taken the greatest care when planting trees and remembered the adage attributed to Mr Veitch of Exeter: "If you plant before Christmas you may tell the trees to grow. If you plant after Christmas you must ask them to grow". I hope my trees will each have a long life; to achieve this it behoves me to maintain and train them to have the balanced growth which is fundamental for their beauty and ability to withstand the elements. The detail and variety of each tree will create a unique atmosphere in the meadow. I have labelled them all and would have liked to add their story and provenance, but this account must suffice for fear that too much information would spoil the peace of the garden. The trees, while withholding their secrets, will however provide friendship for visitors and complement the hedges and plants in the borders.

Chapter 7

Borders - flower power

Dark red paeonies, irises, and pheasant eye narcissi made an audacious display in the neglected garden in 1976; they were worth rescuing from the ground elder so I replanted them temporarily. Ever since these plants have helped perpetuate the charm of the old garden. I studied Russell Page's chapters "On Planting Shrubs" and "On Planting Flowers" in which he emphasises the importance of being sensitive towards plants and their cultural needs. This advice, my style, and the garden's soil and situation would govern my choice of plants. Basically my style is restrained, the soil is alkaline, and the walled garden is on a south-facing slope in somewhat of a frost pocket. I am relieved to forego plants which prefer acid soil and to concentrate on those which will flourish naturally here. Perennials, ferns, grasses, bulbs and annuals will fill borders with their colour, foliage and scent; and shrubs will complete the garden's permanent structure. When a visitor asked me whether my garden was a Gertrude Jekyll garden, I replied emphatically: "No, it's my own garden". I have, of course, been greatly influenced by other gardens but the choice of plants and their associations are my own. My reply to another frequent question "Do you talk to your plants?" is "No, but I know them all".

I have chosen plants I like for positions where they will grow into healthy and shapely specimens I will enjoy tending. I like plants to have space but even so I often plant them too close together. I also like to have a succession of interest and particularly enjoy plants which are at their best in the second half of the year; finally I like to make optimum use of special attributes - scent, foliage and texture. I find plant associations the most difficult aspect of gardening. Perhaps the answer is not to try too hard, after all some of the best associations are those nature makes for herself, and I notice many plants seed themselves in just the right place.

For several years I obstinately resisted owning a copy of the *Plant Finder* because I thought it would take the interest out of searching for plants. But I have succumbed to temptation and consequently enjoy purposeful, if somewhat tame, plant finding expeditions. The book's maps are as useful as the plant lists, and lead to nurseries which might otherwise remain undiscovered. I hope I will never become too selective in my choice of plants, nor become idle about undertaking new planting ideas. Original plants become favourites and replacements will often be just that, so it may be better to maintain enthusiasm by being adventurous and replacing original plants with different varieties. I enjoy propagating plants and seeking less common varieties from nurseries where the owners seem pleased to share a moment and talk. Nursery catalogues become more informative every year and I use them for cross reference and to understand a plant's characteristics. Then, when eventually I bring a plant to the garden, I remember more easily its requirements and how to care for it. Thumbing through catalogues and reference books is also a good exercise in concentration and in overcoming distractions and the temptation to read about other plants. Many plants have travelled with me around the M25 from my parents' garden in Kent, and not just the plant but also support,

Plate 1 Aerial photograph - 1976

Plate 2 Aerial photograph - 1995

Plate 3 Jebel Akhdar, Northern Oman

Plate 4 Desert, Southern Oman

Plate 5 The garden - 1982

Plate 6 The garden - 1995 - similar aspect to plate 5

Plate 7 The view from the terrace

Plate 8 *Pyrus nivalis* - and the entrance to the pond garden

Plate 9 The pond garden

Plate 10 *Alchemilla mollis* (Ladies' Mantle) and *Stipa gigantica*

Plate 11 Hebe with *Rosa* 'Céline Forestier' and *Veronica peduncularis*

Plate 12 The allée with *Polygonatum odoratum* (Solomon's seal), hostas, and *Veronica gentianoides*

Plate 13 The meadow in spring

Plate 14 *Prunus sargentii*

Plate 15 *Juniperus chinensis* 'Aurea'

Plate 16 *Rosa* 'Parkdirektor Riggers'

Plate 17 *Clematis rehderiana* and *C. armandii*

Plate 18 Autumn colour

Plate 19 *Rosa* 'Phyllis Bide'

Plate 20 The box seat *Buxus sempervirens*

Plate 21 Shrub roses

encouragement and helpful advice. An uncle once commented that a Daniell never goes anywhere by car without a plant.

In front of the cottage and garage, where there are varied aspects and a twenty metre length of west facing wall, I grow *Iris stylosa*, *Primula* spp., and *Erigeron karvinskiansus* in narrow borders beneath climbing shrubs. Beside the front door the colours of *Clematis orientalis* 'Bill Mackenzie', which has flower petals like orange peel and grey seed heads, complement the door's grey paintwork. *Lonicera nitida* 'Baggesen's Gold', a grey leafed rock rose *helianthemum nummularium* 'Wisley Primrose' and *Choysia ternata* grow well as evergreens and scent from the latter drifts into the cottage. In a partly shaded border on my southern boundary *Helleborus orientalis*, *Fuchsia triphylla*, annuals, and *Cornus alba* 'Elegantissima' with its red winter stems, grow above *Persicaria affine*, and *Symphytum grandiflorum*, but beware, symphytum is a very invasive plant.

In front of the small shed by the steps leading down to the cottage I grow myrtle *Myrtus communis* which flowers in August, and rosemary *Rosmarinus officinalis* which I cannot help but brush against throughout the year. In a most inhospitable position which the sun never reaches but where a tiny wren chooses to nest, scented *Mahonia x media* 'Lionel Fortescue' flowers faithfully each winter. Around the base of the Washington apple tree I have a small rockery where several cultivars of *Erica carnea* flourish, together with *Geranium subcaulescens* with its deep red flowers, variegated thyme *Thymus* 'Doone Valley', *Aubrietia* spp., *Tanacetum herderi* with its feathery grey foliage, *Silene uniflora*, pinks *Dianthus* 'Mrs Sinkins', crocuses *C. chrysanthus* 'Cream Beauty' and *Primula* spp. I have a favourite and prominent spot under the apple tree where each summer I grow lime coloured nicotiana that flowers for weeks on end in partial shade. In a nearby dark corner knotweed *Persicaria affine*, snowdrops *Galanthus nivalis*, white bluebells *Hyacinthoides hispanica* 'Alba' and lily of the valley *Convallaria majalis* each flower in their turn, and individual dwarf box shrubs mark the entrance to the walled garden through the wrought iron gate.

By this gate the wall's mellow red and vitreous slate coloured bricks reflect the colours in the flowers of the lacecap hydrangea *H.* 'Lanarth White'; it is a good example of a plant I like in a place where it flourishes. Around it *Clematis cirrhosa* 'Balearica' with its pale freckled flowers, wintersweet *Chimonanthus praecox*, which took eight years to flower, Christmas box *Sarcococca confusa*, *Abeliophyllum dissectum* with its fragile pink flowers, and *Daphne mezereum alba* all contribute their winter colour and scent. Among these plants *Itea ilicifolia* which develops striking tassels in late summer, and variegated *Trachelospermum asiaticum*, both of which have interesting foliage, associate well with the flowers of *Clematis* 'Lord Nevill' which are a deep blue colour in July and August. At the northern end of the wall penstemons and *Felicia echinata*, with its pink daisy flowers, fill spaces at the base of the old trained pear trees. In early spring aconites, snowdrops and narcissi provide a cheerful welcome which red roses and catmint continue throughout the summer. In front of the garage another rosemary covers the central pillar, but it is a short-lived variety so I have a replacement ready. Nearby I am training a bay tree into a conical shape in one of the very few tubs in the garden, and under the garage eaves the pale yellow flowers of St John's Wort *Hypericum calycinum* show well against the brown walls. Although it is vulnerable to rust, hypericum is a good ground cover plant which I cut back hard in spring when new growth appears. In shade on the northern side of the garage *Tolmeia menziesii*, epimediums including *E. pinnatum colchium*, *E. pubigerum* and *E. x rubrum*, and *Bergenia cordifolia* spread themselves; against the wall above them *Schizophragma hydrangeoides* (similar to *Hydrangea petiolaris*) should flower in late summer. A white flowering currant, *Ribes sanguineum* 'Tydeman's White', and the heavily scented viburnum *V. bodnantense* 'Dawn' are also growing well here in the shade. The area in front of the cottage and around the garage is a garden in itself with varied aspects and opportunities for planting; in the walled garden there are many more.

The paved area, or sunken terrace, on the eastern side of the cottage is another small garden in which there are two planting areas. In the smaller, the size of a paving slab, yellow panicles of lady's mantle *Alchemilla mollis* combine with the golden seed heads of the tall grass *Stipa gigantica* to make a delicate display - their foliage could hardly be in greater contrast (Plate 10). In the larger area edged with box cuttings from the mother hedge, a dozen delicately scented white roses R. 'Margaret Merrill' flourish; here also, in spring, a brilliant display of scarlet tulips T. Appledoorn precedes the roses. Against the cottage the climbing rose R. 'Parkdirektor Riggers', with scarlet flowers and attractive serrated foliage, thrives and remains healthy throughout the summer (Plate 16). *Potentilla fruticosa* 'Abbotswood' and *Mahonia aquifolium* enjoy sun and shade at the edge of the terrace with nerines *N. bowdenii*, white and blue sisyrynchiums *S.* 'Californian Skies' and 'Pole Star', *Saxifraga x urbium* 'London Pride' and a mophead hydrangea *H.* 'Mme Emile Mouillère'. *Erigeron karvinskianus*, with its seemingly everlasting daisylike flowers, and yellow *Corydalis lutea* have seeded themselves in and around the steps and softened them. I am training *Cotoneaster horizontalis* in front of the riser of the lowest step; it is an accommodating plant that responds to careful attention. At either side of this lowest step, with dwarf *Persicaria affine* spreading at their base, I cosset two lemon scented verbena *Aloysia triphylla* for their foliage. A small apricot coloured rose R. 'Anthea Fortescue', given to me by Anthea and her husband Tim, has a special position near the cottage. *Lilium candidum* also flood the cottage with their scent on a summer's evening.

In a raised and shaded border on the southern side of the terrace *Hosta sieboldii*, Solomon's seal *Polygonatum odoratum*, *Euphorbia polychroma*, *Dicentra exima* 'alba', cranesbills *Geranium cinereum* and *G. dalmaticum*, *Anenome seemanii*, and *Helleborus niger* make an attractive display with their foliage. They are preceded by tulips and the powder blue flower spikes of *Veronica gentianoides* which spreads harmlessly to cover the ground. At the back of the border the pale pink flowers of the thornless rose R. 'Zepherine Drouhin' look cool against the flint wall. At one end of the border a variegated *Euonymous fortunei* 'Silver Queen' has grown into an attractive mound at the base of the beech hedge. All these plants around the eastern side of the cottage are ones I like in situations they like - consequently they flourish.

At the furthest end of the allée from the cottage, at the base of Hebe's statue, several hebe plants grow well and the repeat flowering rose R. 'Céline Forrestier' climbs against the flint wall; the rose's soft yellow blooms add to an already attractive picture (Plate 11). Here also, around the base of the Lady Henniker apple tree, snowdrops and *Cyclamen coum* flower bravely in winter and in summer tall allium *A. nigrum* reinforce the tree's striking framework. Against the flint boundary wall the pink thornless rose R. 'Kathleen Harrop' makes a delicate display in June and again in late September. Below the rose catmint *Nepeta x faassenii* with ribbed grey foliage complements the flints in the wall. In future I hope a white wisteria will grow along wires at a higher level and create privacy for my neighbours.

The corner border at the top of the incline is full of plants with strong colours and interesting names: the scarlet rose R. 'Sultan Qaboos', the crimson dahlia *D.* 'Bishop of Llandaff' with deeply incised dark foliage, maroon hollyhocks *Althaea rosea* from Oman, and blue *Salvia patens*. Pinks *Dianthus* 'Mrs Sinkins' and summer annuals, including the unusual *Cleome spinosa* with its spidery flowers, and blue *Cynoglossum amabile* 'Firmament' fill any gaps. Tulips and wallflowers will have had the border to themselves in spring together with *Euchryphia x nymansiensis* 'Nymansay', a beautiful late flowering summer shrub. I am giving it every encouragement but it is reluctant to become established; if only it knew I have a replacement in the nursery. Variegated arabis *A. fernandi-coburgii* breaks over the paving here and brings light and detail into a dark space at the base of the yew hedge; perceptive gardeners admire it.

The herbaceous borders that provide such a long sequence of colour and interest look best from the seat against the flint wall. The northern of the two borders is backed by a yew hedge and enjoys sunshine all day; the southern border is more shaded and is backed by a beech hedge. In the northern border blue, grey, and pink colours, with some white and many shades of green, make an attractive show, while to the south yellow, red, pink and shades of white and green combine well. There is nothing new in this selection of colours but I am pleased to have discovered it and the harmonious result. Among the plants a polyantha rose R. 'Nathalie Nypels' deserves special mention. It has pale clusters of pink flowers continuously from June to November; grows just one metre high and is usually remarkably free of disease. As one flower fades another always seems to be waiting to burst open. Nathalie Nypels must have been a delightful person for such a rose to be named after her.

Two rose borders, each with twelve R. 'Beautiful Britain', backed by yew hedging are either side of the entrance to the pond garden. This floribunda rose is another healthy variety which has a succession of tomato red flowers throughout the summer. In front of the yew the rose's colour and polished foliage are set off to best advantage; I am not surprised that in 1983 it was chosen as Rose of the Year. Similar coloured tulips *T.* 'Gordon Cooper' fill the borders in spring and lavender which grows amongst them conceals the rose bushes' bare stems.

The plants in the pond garden are principally blue, pink, and white, but I have included other strong colours. Red lobelia *L. cardinalis*, yellow marsh marigolds *Caltha palustris* and flag irises *I. pseudocorus* grow as marginal plants in the pond and add strength with their colours. A ceanothus *C.* 'Autumnal Blue', clematis *C. viticella* and the rose R. 'Pompon de Paris' clothe the wall; the tiny pink flowers of the latter sometimes brave the winter cold. The narrow variegated leaves of *Miscanthus sinensis* 'Variegatus' contrast with hostas and red tulips adding brilliant colour in the spring. The branches of *Cornus alternifolia* 'Argentea' grow in tiers like a wedding cake in one corner, with lesser periwinkle and purple bugle beneath them. In another corner *Weigela florida* 'Variegata' is the principal plant surrounded by *Caryopteris x clandonensis* 'Heavenly Blue', two ceratostigmas *C. griffithi* and *C. willmottianum*,

Anaphalis triplivernis, Veronica peduncularis and a small leafed variegated myrtle *Myrtus communis* 'Microphylla Variegata'. Elsewhere nerine lilies, fuchsias, eryngium, and irises give of their best, and the soft red flowers of the water lilies *Nymphae* 'Escarboucle' and 'Rose Arey' - the loveliest of flowers - bloom from June to October.

Anemone blanda flower throughout February and March around the base of *Magnolia x loebneri* 'Merrill' in the main lawn; in a corner border beyond these are plants with matt textured foliage, but of course there are exceptions. The border has come together well, whatever the plants, and it takes little maintenance. The golden juniper *Juniperus chinensis* 'Aurea', with a background of yew and surrounded with a mass of old English lavender *L. angustifolia,* is the principal plant, but *Potentilla fruticosa* 'Abbotswood', *Buddleia fallowiana* 'Lochinch' with foliage like grey felt, the grey leafed *Dorycnium hirsutum* and *Hebe armstrongii* with its cord-like foliage are amongst others in the border. The deep red paeonies *Paeonia officinalis* and blue irises *I. Pseudocorus* that I rescued from the strangulating ground elder *Aegopodium podograria,* and the pale yellow *Paeonia mlokosewitschii* 'Molly the Witch', for whose flowers I waited eight years, also flourish here. This corner border is similar in size and shape to the border by the black cast iron pump in the northeast corner at the top of the slope, but each border contains very different plants.

In the border near the pump a fastigiate yew is the focal point at the end of the northeasterly vista from the cottage. The yew with a tall euphorbia *E. characias* and variegated cornus *C. alba* 'Elegantissima' make an attractive group, but my chief purpose for the planting here is autumn interest and colour (Plate 18). *Rosa rubrifolia* with its glaucous purple foliage, small pink flowers and mass of red hips overshadows *Spiraea japonica* 'Goldflame', michaelmas daisies *Aster novae-angliae, Sedum* 'Autumn Joy' and *Acanthus mollis. Rubus cockburnianus,* with its lime green foliage and white stems in winter, stands above epimediums, dwarf polygonum *Persicaria affine,* and *Omphalodes cappadocica* 'Starry Eyes'. The foliage of most of these plants provides double value with their display of pale green shades in early summer.

Nearby some very satisfactory plants grow against the flint wall and in the paving. A valuable rose R. 'Phyllis Bide' - the Bide family were nurserymen not far away in Farnham - flourishes behind the seat (Plate 19). The rose's apricot coloured buds, small and tight, break into compact semi-double flowers throughout the summer. From a distance these blooms look like flints and reflect those in the wall. R. 'Phyllis Bide' grows strongly but not too vigorously, and vies with R. 'Nathalie Nypels' for beauty, good health and continuity of flowering.

Behind the black pump, in the sunniest corner of the garden, the grey green foliage and yellow pineapple scented flowers of Moroccan broom *Cytisus battandieri* are shown to best effect against the flint wall. Every year in August I cut this shrub hard back and without fail it responds well with strong growth. Beneath it the pink trumpets of *Crinum x powellii* and its white counterpart are valuable late summer flowers and nearby a small-leafed myrtle bears its delicate white flowers. In spring lily-of-the-valley growing in shade fill the air with their scent, and tulips, wallflowers, and forget-me-nots thrive until cosmos take their place in high summer. In this corner, which not so long ago was full of garden debris, strong pink hollyhocks from Oman complete the picture beside the grey gate that opens into the meadow.

Wherever there is a gate I have a scented shrub beside it, and by the meadow gate a winter flowering honeysuckle *Lonicera fragrantissima* flowers bravely on the north side of the wall; the flowers invite close inspection and then the fragrance is readily appreciated. Beside this honeysuckle two viburnums flourish: the well known winter flowering *V. tinus*, and the not so well known *V. plicatum* 'Mareisii'. The latter is a good architectural shrub and in summer bears a mass of white flowers - mine deserves more space.

In the meadow I have planted four principal areas: a narrow border with climbing plants against the north side of the wall, a large border which I started as a reserve for plants I could not fit into the walled garden, specimen shrubs amongst the trees and plants around the observatory. In addition the greenhouse in the nursery area is a carnation house where these floriferous plants produce excellent blooms for ten months of the year.

The border on the north side of the garden wall has been one of the most interesting to plant. I studied and cross-checked many lists of plants for shade before I selected plum, pear, cherry and blackberry for one third of the space, roses and clematis for another third and other climbers for the remainder. Amongst the last group is one of the best plants in the garden - the fuchsia-flowered gooseberry *Ribes speciosum*. It has pendulous flowers similar to a fuchsia which bloom for nearly six weeks, its leaves are similar to a gooseberry, and it has thin but strong pointed spines along its stems. I am training it as a fan and it has grown to about three metres. Nearby is a variegated pyracantha *P.* 'Sparkler' - another star performer - which although reputed to be tender survives without protection. Its small leaves become attractively tinged with red in autumn. A variegated euonymous *E. fortunei* 'Silver Pillar' fills a narrow gap satisfactorily and a variegated cotoneaster *C. horizontalis* 'Variegatus' spreads vertically to cover the wall.

Five clematis flourish against this north-facing wall. *C.* 'Marie Boisselot' (*C.* 'Mme le Coultre') with large white flowers; pink flowered *C.* 'Nelly Moser'; *C.* 'Jackmanii' with its large purple flowers; *C.* 'Polish Spirit' that continues to flower into November and *C. macropetala* 'Markham's Pink' which has pink bell-shaped flowers in the spring. They are all treasures and seem to remain in bloom and retain their freshness for longer than the clematis in full sun on the south side of the wall. Roses occupy the remainder of the space.

Three roses do particularly well but a fourth, *R.* 'Mermaid', struggles as it seeks light; I hope *C.* 'Polish Spirit' will cover its rather scraggy legs. *R.* 'Danse du Feu' is spreading as I intend round Persephone's plaque; she would have enjoyed the red blooms that make such a cheerful picture. *R.* 'Madame Alfred Carrière' grows vigorously at the other end of the border where its strong scent stops visitors in their tracks. *R.* 'New Dawn' has yet to establish itself but my hopes match the catalogue description: "... a shapely rose with pale pink scented buds". Ground cover plants flourish at the base of the wall; among them are: epimediums, *Tiarella cordifolia*, *Brunnera macrophylla*, *Omphalodes cappodocica*, *Vinca minor*, *Persicaria affine*, *Lamium maculatum* 'Silver Beacon' and *Viola labradorica*. Variegated ground elder, *Aegopodium podagraria* 'Variegatum', well contained on three sides and mown on the fourth, is a most effective ground cover and brings light to the border. Ferns also are becoming established but taking their time. The shuttlecock fern *Matteuccia struthiopteris* is attractive when its fresh young fronds unfurl in spring, and the hart's tongue fern *Asplenium scolopendrium* with its shiny foliage is showing promise. A variegated cornus *C. alba* 'Spaethii' and a bamboo *Thalmocalamnus spathiflora* fill corner spaces at either end of this seventy-five metre long narrow border. I have laid a 'mowing strip' its full length and the whole is fast becoming a fine sight set against the wall's mellow bricks and grey lichen.

The wide shrub border, in contrast with the wall border, is open to all possible sunshine. Low growing plants including rock roses *helianthemum nummularium*, cistus *C. x corbariensis*, a number of cranesbills *Geranium spp.*, *Euphorbia myrsinites* and *Tiarella cordifolia* spread over the stone edging. Purple bugle *Ajuga reptans* 'Purpurea' flourishes wherever I put it, and the poached egg plant *Limnanthes douglassii* flowers at least twice in the year and spreads its fern-like foliage in a kindly way. I like grasses and *Carex riparia* 'Bowles Golden', *Molinia caerulea* and *Festuca glauca* make a group while on a larger scale at the other end of the border a pampas *Cortaderia* 'Pumila', which grows to only two metres, makes a fine display in late autumn sunshine. Two of David Austen's New English roses, *R.* 'Winchester Cathedral' and *R.* 'St Swithun', bloom throughout the summer and link the garden with the Cathedral and one of its patron saints. An attractive late flowering honeysuckle *Lonicera periclymenum* 'Serotina' with its dark red and pink flowers is growing into a large mound around a tree stump, and the variegated foliage and black or red stems of three dogwoods make a valuable show throughout the year. *Elaeagnus x ebbingei*, *Abelia x grandiflora*, *Syringa vulgaris* 'Mme Lemoine', *Hibiscus syriacus*, *Kolkwitzia amabilis* and *Exochorda macrantha* 'The Bride', with its mass of white blossom in the spring, will soon grow together and make a screen along the north side of the border. Other notable plants are variegated privet *Ligustrum ovalifolium* 'Argenteum', *Daphne odora* and *Elaeagnus angustifolia* 'Quicksilver' which should grow rapidly into a small tree with yellow flowers smelling of balsam. I like this border not only for its plants but also for its generous size and the space it provides. Even so I have run out of space and planted more shrubs as specimens elsewhere in the meadow.

The crimson autumn foliage of *Euonymous alatus* attracted me so it is now in a prominent position in the meadow; *Philadelphus* 'Belle Etoile' with its heavily scented white and purple flowers is nearby and *Cornus controversa* 'Eddie's White Wonder' - another Jenkyn Place plant - is not far away. I have planted a smoke bush *Cotinus coggyria* amongst some silver birch trees; as a mature shrub I can think of few others as attractive. *Elaeagnus x ebbingei,* which I chose for its green and grey foliage and heavily scented small flowers in October, and *Viburnum fragrans* were early introductions to the meadow. So there are good reasons for having planted all these extra shrubs and no doubt I will find equally good reasons for any more I introduce. Four shrub roses grow well: R. 'Californica Plena', R. 'Anne of Gerstein', R. *pomifera* and R. *xanthina* 'Canary Bird'. The first three are large specimens with attractive pink flowers and R. *pomifera* has a good scent. R. 'Canary Bird' is an early yellow rose that I admire for its delicate foliage but I never had a place for it until friends gave me one. Three R. *rugosa* 'Alba' are quickly making a good clump near the centre of the meadow. They are valuable plants not only for their white scented flowers, but also for their red hips in autumn. Opposite them I intend that three small box bushes should grow into large mounds. In a far corner of the meadow, where I let the nettles grow for the benefit of butterflies, I have planted a honeysuckle *Lonicera periclymenum* 'Graham Stuart Thomas'; it will spread freely and I look forward to seeing it smothered in butterflies. Finally, round the base of the sundial I am growing camomile which should release its scent while visitors stand on it and pause to read the time.

The flowers and shrubs in the meadow are a collection which I often admire from the observatory which is surrounded with a lilac from Wales, a juniper from Ireland and a Spanish broom. These are interlopers in my garden which is meant to be in keeping with the surroundings; but they are welcome.

In the walled garden the border in front of the south-facing wall is a gardener's delight. It is the first border I cleared of ground elder and I keep it narrow so that climbing plants are easy to reach and train; there seems little point in growing plants against such a fine wall if they are not kept close to it. In those early days I noticed an offer of attractive climbing plants in a weekend paper: *Teuchrium fruticans* with its grey foliage and pale blue flowers; *Fremontodendron californicum* with deep yellow flowers;

Trachelospermum asiaticum with highly scented white flowers in July; and *Actinidia kolomikta* with green, white and pink foliage which is so vulnerable to frost. I ordered these and have added *Ceanothus* 'Puget's blue', the yellow rose R. 'Golden Showers'; a white japonica *Chaenomeles speciosa* 'Nivalis'; and two clematis *C. armandii* and *C. rehderiana* which make a most attractive combination (Plate 17). I cut back the *C. armandii* hard as soon as it has finished flowering in the spring, and then enjoy its fresh new foliage. At the end of the summer the *C. rehderiana,* with its panicles of primrose bell-shaped flowers, comes into its own and continues to flower for several weeks. Special sweet peas, *Lathyrus chloranthus* and *L. sativus* - with their respective yellow and blue flowers - enjoy warmth from the wall, and *Geranium procurrens* with its small purple flowers scrambles around; but beware of this energetic plant which takes root wherever it touches the ground. Another variegated cotoneaster fills a gap and a small pomegranate *Punica granatum,* which I doubt will ever bear fruit, contributes its shiny foliage to the scene. Nearby *Coronilla glauca* 'Citrina' flowers for most of the year, and competes to be the best plant in the garden. Beneath the climbers ground cover plants spread over a stone edging strip which prevents them being mown. A*rtemisia* 'Powis Castle', two dwarf day lilies *Hemerocallis minor* and *H. multiflora,* catmint *Nepeta × fassenii* and *Nerine bowdenii* continue their colour and interest into the autumn. Dwarf narcissi *N.* 'Jack Snipe' and *N.* 'Jenny' *Ipheion uniflorum,* snowdrops, erysimums *E. alpinum* and *E. linifolium,* and *Iris laevigata* contribute their colour in spring. The complete border is best seen from an angle because its width and variety are too much for the eye to absorb frontally. Across the grass a solitary variegated *Pittisporum garnettii,* which sometimes has scented garnet coloured flowers shaped like tiny round buttons, grows freely and makes a peaceful picture in a corner backed by dark green yew.

The remaining section of old box hedge dictates the size and shape of the border on the right approaching the wrought iron gate. Here, against the brick wall are a climbing rose R. 'Iceberg', and *Clematis* 'Alba Luxurians' which has delicate white flowers, the tips of the petals tinged with green. Old fashioned shrub roses, irises, foxgloves, day lilies and white *Anemone x hybrida* 'Honorine Joubert' also flourish. Some of the roses are repeat flowering and their blooms join the anenomes' in September. Because it is awkward getting close enough to appreciate their scent I chose each rose for its shape, size and colour. *Rosa* 'Rose de Rescht', *R.* 'Mme Hardy', *R.* 'Isphahan', *R.* 'Penelope', *R.* 'Felicite Parmentier' and *R.* 'Maiden's Blush' are all names which contribute to the essentially female character of this border which I regret does not remain at its best for longer, but in high summer it is as beautiful as any rose border.

All of these plants and many more provide the interest throughout the year I set out to achieve; but to look their best the borders in which they flourish are set within well maintained lawns or meadow grass. There is, however, more to creating this setting than just cutting the grass.

Chapter 8

Grass - green peace

When I laid turf in front of the cottage, where potatoes had earlier helped to clear the ground, the transformation was immediate. That success in 1979 gave me confidence and enthusiasm to press on. I bought my first rotary mower and admired the cut it gave the grass; neglect was banished and care became my watchword. The only garden sight which dejects me is an unkempt lawn; put that right and all is well.

While I changed the shape of the earth in the walled garden I set the topsoil aside and later returned it carefully in preparation for sowing the lawns during the summer of 1983. I used Manhattan seed which was the first perennial rye grass bred specifically to be hard wearing, slow growing and disease resistant; it included genetic material from grass growing in the harsh conditions of Central Park, New York. In the kinder environment of my garden its characteristics contribute to good lawns - if not luxury then certainly utility grade.

One of my important lawn management tasks which encourages strong root growth is an autumn feed with plenty of phosphates but lacking in nitrogen. Another task is repairing damaged edges and worn areas. A half moon edging tool, a turfing iron and a plank are the simple items required for this work. After cutting an outline in the turf it is satisfying to slide the turfing iron under the grass roots and then to roll up a section of turf of even thickness. It is even more satisfying to re-lay the roll so that the new piece may bind with the surrounding turf, and the result look as if it could never have been any other way. I rest the lawns during winter although in mild and dry weather I sometimes brush away the wormcasts and cut the grass with the blades set high. The first major lawn task when the ground dries in the spring is to roll and level the surface after the effects of frost. I reckoned a ride-on mower I won as first prize in a 'best big lawn' competition would make light work of towing a roller but, because I could not find a competition with a roller as first prize, I made my own. I filled a section of yellow gas pipe with concrete and in it set a length of scaffolding pole as an axle casing. This heavy cylinder, held in an oak frame, trundles effectively behind my tractor. I was not so creative with equipment to aerate the lawn and bought a device with a devilish array of spikes to drag behind the tractor. Sometimes green woodpeckers aerate the ground for me while they search for ants. I can get quite close to them, but they are sensitive birds and seem to have a planned escape route; suddenly they are up and away in their characteristic undulating flight. Scarifying is the next task and I usually manage to dislodge quantities of thatch; walking barefoot on the lawn afterwards is similar to walking on the very best quality carpet. Hand weeding, and feeding a little and often throughout the summer, ensure healthy lawns provided I mow regularly and there is adequate rain. I refrain from watering grass because any lasting effect requires volumes of water. So much for the care and maintenance of the lawns.

The western section of the meadow became of special interest when I decided to grow wild flowers there. I was inspired to do this while I enjoyed a summer walk from the cottage along the Pilgrim's Way where chalkland wild flowers flourished in the verges. For a season I cut and collected the grass to reduce the fertility of the ground. Meanwhile a local nursery sold me thumb size wildflower plugs. I grew these on with some of my own seedlings and in the autumn planted them in the meadow. In future I will cut the grass there until the beginning of June, and in the Autumn. I look forward to a meadow of summer wildflowers - harebell, chickory, scabious, and cranesbill - which should multiply until they find their balance, but I know this is easier said than done.

In the eastern section of the meadow I have planted many bulbs - too many too close together. The effect is exciting from the time the earliest yellow trumpeted narcissi *N.* 'Peeping Tom' flower in February, until late April when the pheasant eye variety *N. poeticus* var. *recurvus* appear. In one area there are masses of snowdrops with winter aconites, grape hyacinths, and wood anemones: in another, near a colony of cowslips, some bluebells under silver birch; and behind the evergreen oak hedge fritillaries *Fritillaria meleagris* bear their delicate blooms. On a bright spring morning the meadow is a fearless sight when the bulbs hold their heads high and look towards the sun (Plate 13). In contrast after frost they droop for a while and look sad but soon recover. I cut the long meadow grass in early July after dead heading the bulbs' faded blooms and waiting for their foliage to die. No sooner have I done this than buttercups flourish en masse and create a scene which would thrill an impressionist painter; even more so when poppy blooms add their grace and colour.

The meadow is a good place to observe the many birds which enjoy the surroundings. Some, like the swallows, make me look up and bring the wide sky into my gardening life. Ducks, geese and swans in flight sometimes seem to be stacked overhead as if waiting for their turn in the flightpath before landing on the river. Pheasants call from the fields and hedges around the garden, owls hoot from the trees along the railway embankment, and rooks quarrel in the tall beech trees around Abbey House where woodpeckers also hammer. The dawn chorus in May is a concert, as is the birds' evensong that I sometimes listen to from the observatory in the meadow. I enjoy this evensong most because I am in a mood to relax as opposed to struggling to sleep through the dawn. In winter the garden birds become even more a part of my garden, whether they be the tits, robins, nuthatches and finches I feed and encourage to nest in boxes, or the blackbirds and thrushes which massacre windfall apples on the terrace. Throughout the garden birds enjoy the place and make a spirited contribution to it and my work. But, for now, back to the mower.

I enjoy mowing the lawns regularly and find truth in the Reverend Edward Budding's statement when he promoted his first lawn mower in 1830: "Country gentlemen may find in using my machine themselves, an amusing, useful and healthy exercise". I would only add that I find it even more rewarding if the machinery is well maintained and used intelligently. Essential to the upkeep of all my grass is efficient machinery. Little is more infuriating than the mower that fails during a tight schedule of grass cutting; it is all the more infuriating when the fault is mine. I have used a great variety of grass cutters since hacking back the old cabbage stalks, thistles and bramble thickets with a flail until now when I strive to make a close cut sward. A ride-on mower with its wide cut, a good cylinder mower, and a strong rotary are my current stable and serve me well. The cylinder mower has transformed my grass cutting into lawn mowing - just as the Reverend Budding forecast it would. The scissors action of the blades gives a fine cut and I enjoy mowing the lawns in every direction while the engine chugs away, making that summer sound so characteristic of parks and large gardens. I usually leave the grass cuttings uncollected to return their goodness to the ground; with regular scarifying this must be the best practice and saves emptying awkward grassboxes. When I mow for a super plus result edging strips along the front of borders, careful use of a strimmer and the minimum of turns, halts and reverses all help to save valuable time. In the meadow the ride-on mower makes short shrift of the grass. While I follow the meadow paths I often recall the outline of the house with a sloping roof which I drew as a puzzle at school; the object was to avoid going over the same line twice.

Well maintained grass complements beautiful flowers except the most beautiful of all - the lilies in the pond.

Chapter 9

The Pond - a Golden Section

The pond is a garden in its own right where plants, fish and a variety of water creatures flourish. They enjoy the nutritious clear water and the oxygen created as the water tumbles from the fountain. In the pond a dozen red blooms of water lilies *Nymphaea* 'Escarboucle' and *N.* 'Rose Arey' are a brilliant and refreshing sight for the sorest eyes.

I began to consider the detail of the pond not in the desert but while working in London where a small pond in Whitehall Gardens beside the Thames Embankment inspired me. I admired this discreet pond and listened to the delicate sound of its waterspout tinkling above the roar of London traffic. The pond's proportions are a Golden Section and it became the model for my own pond which is formal, insofar as any pond with all its life and activity can be formal, and a study in perfection - well almost.

I dug a large hole, lined it with sand and old carpet, and made a firm surround for the stone edging. I placed a butyl liner over the hole, led a hose to it and wondered whether, when I turned the water on, the liner would stretch or collapse into the hole. It stretched perfectly as the water inched upwards and the hole became a pond. But I should have been more careful when laying the edging stones. The water surface is level but the edges are not. I have tried to mitigate my mistake with marginal plants - bullrushes *Typha latifolia,* water forget-me-not *Myosotis palustris* and marsh marigolds *Caltha palustris,* all of which have made phenomenal growth, but most annoyingly I know the levels are wrong. I have no excuse except my enthusiasm to fill the pond.

During my search for a suitable centrepiece I saw many beautiful ornaments. I arrived at one dealer's showroom simultaneously with a cormorant - a lead one grasping an eel; it was exactly what I was searching for. Of course the price was above my budget but I bought the ornament and carried it home by train. It is now the centrepiece of the pond where it stands fifty centimetres high on an upturned rhubarb forcing-pot and conceals a submersible pump. I enjoy venturing over the water on a scaffolding plank to adjust the height of the waterspout from the mouth of the eel. The spout is mesmerising as it rises, tumbles back on itself and shatters on the cormorant's back. Sparkling water droplets then dash across the surface of the pond until they lose their momentum and collapse. The sound of my fountain, unlike that in the London pond, competes only with birdsong and croaking frogs.

In the grip of spring fever frogs and toads come to the pond to lay eggs and leave their spawn. Late one February evening, after a high speed 'awayday' to Paris on Eurostar, I returned to the garden to hear frogs mating in the pond; the primitive sound of their activity filled the garden and the cottage. I could only marvel. The resulting tadpoles will be voracious scavengers and help maintain a healthy pond until, as tiny creatures, they survey their world from the lily pads, just like Beatrix Potter's Jeremy Fisher, and then migrate in search of a dank home elsewhere in the garden. I have laid a ramp to assist their migration and have a notice ready for visitors: "Beware of the frogs".

Birds also enjoy the pond. Early one morning I saw a heron eyeing his catch but I scared him and he flew away languidly never yet to return. I have also seen a brilliant and dashing kingfisher perch momentarily on the inert fountain; that was an exceptional moment. Calls from waterfowl, living amongst the reeds and tussocks of the riverbank, join the garden chorus and make the pond seem truly in keeping with its surroundings. Water creatures have established their community amongst the lilies, water weed and marginal plants. I introduced six lively goldfish whose progeny flourish, always looking sleek and friendly. Watching them and noticing their different colours, shapes and sizes - particularly their tails - is time consuming but worth every minute, as are minutes spent admiring the brilliance of dragon and damselflies which hover and dash in all directions, chasing insects and maybe just for joy. These creatures will have incubated in the pond and their presence is the surest sign it is healthy.

If the pond had no purpose other than to grow water lilies even then it would be worthwhile. The lilies I have selected flower brilliantly from June to October, while their handsome foliage provides shade which denies green algae the light needed for their survival. Waterweed *Elodea canadensis* also flourishes and not only creates oxygen but, by competing with the algae for important nutrients, helps to maintain clear water. When the water temperature increases in May and the weed begins to grow the algae perish and the water becomes clear - sometimes overnight. Later in the year decayed leaves and lily pads are potentially harmful and I remove them before they create sludge. Ice is another hazard so I make a hole for a wide tube which allows oxygen to enter the water and other gases to escape. Meanwhile the fish do not give anything away and continue to enjoy the pond's deepest water.

The pond is a feature with an amazing variety of life and growth to watch and understand. I sometimes study it closely in shade at ground level and notice the sparkling life of many creatures going about their unique purpose; this puts me right in nature's pocket. However, as Rudyard

Kipling wrote "...such gardens are not made by singing 'Oh how beautiful', and sitting in the shade". Fruit and vegetables will not grow on their own.

Chapter 10

Fruit and Veg - produce

I will not forget that the garden had always been a fruit and vegetable garden until I found it, but then only two very old vines in the dilapidated vinehouse showed signs of care and attention. "Ichabod"[5]. The glory which had departed from the garden left behind not only unique charm but also unkempt apple and pear trees, an adventurous fig and a withering peach tree. Gooseberry bushes, a colony of stout rhubarb, and remains of previous years' cabbages struggled to survive around a weedy asparagus bed. I am glad to have seen the place in that state and although I have created a very different garden 'fruit and veg' is a significant element of it. Four of the original apple trees are as valuable for their fruit as for their impact on my design, the vines are irreplaceable, the rhubarb is nourishing and in the meadow I have planted more fruit trees and dug a vegetable garden.

The Bramley is the finest and most shapely of the four landmark apple trees. Its apples are easy to pick if I climb up and get amongst them, although some beyond my reach eventually fall onto the terrace with a thud, a noise which has become another characteristic garden sound. Lady

---

[5] 1 Samuel Ch 4 v 21. "And she named the child Ichabod, saying, the glory is departed from Israel..."

Henniker's apple was raised on the Henniker family estate in Suffolk in about 1850; my tree is smaller than the Bramley and bears a dual-purpose apple I pick in late September. It keeps well until Christmas, but tastes best eaten immediately from the tree - preferably before breakfast. Washington is another uncommon dual-purpose apple raised in Washington County, New York in about 1840; my tree was extremely neglected but is responding to a programme of renovation and forms healthy fruit buds. The fourth tree, Cox's Orange Pippin, is very prone to disease but it is a shapely specimen in front of the potting shed and a most useful prop for coats and equipment: so no matter that it does not bear well.

The three pear trees trained against the west-facing wall have character and are old, perhaps one hundred and fifty years old. The Royal Horticultural Society identified one tree, with the label dated 1850 on the wall behind it, as The Vicar of Winkfield but I believe it could be - as labelled - Beurre de Rance. Beside it Comice is a gnarled old espalier that has delicious pears, and Nouveau Poiteau is another, bearing a dessert pear for picking at the end of October. I am enjoying training a new variety Concorde as an espalier against a north-facing wall. Pears require timely harvesting and most careful handling and storing - even in a refrigerator - but bringing them to perfection is rewarding.

Fruit and Veg - produce

Harry Baker, the acknowledged fruit expert who recently retired from the Royal Horticultural Society, boosted my fruit growing interests during a visit. He came with **Periwinkle Productions** who used the garden to make sections of several gardening videos. Harry gave of his unequalled knowledge in a kind and instructive way. I learnt an enormous amount from him, especially about the effects and benefits of correct pruning. He planted cordon, espalier and bush apple trees in my young orchard - Aunt Dorothy's orchard - and I look forward to his inspection of them.

I think William Bunney would be glad to know that one hundred and fifty years after he won his medal at a Horticultural Society of London show held in Winchester, fruit from his garden has won prizes at a Royal Horticultural Society show in London. Whereas he would have enjoyed good local gardening talk after his Winchester show I enjoyed an exciting visit to a very different type of show at Olympia - the Apple Macintosh Computer Expo. Inside Olympia the world of computers seemed - like horticulture - creative and enormous, but I felt lost amongst the bright lights and background of **electronic noise**. Everywhere a younger generation spoke rapidly in an alien language about computer technology. During one hightech talk I heard amongst the soundbites: "...sweeping along an axial path" and for a moment imagined I was at a horticultural show or even in my orchard.

The orchard replaces one marked on a map dated 1869 at the western end of the meadow. There is no trace of that orchard but the position seemed ideal for planting my own. I chose nine apple trees on M26 dwarfing rootstock; they will pollinate each other and fruit over a long period; the first to ripen in August should be Discovery and the last in November Tydeman's Late Orange. I am glad to have included amongst the trees in this orchard some varieties I removed from the garden in 1982. I did not let the young trees fruit their first year, in the second they produced only a meagre crop, and Jack Frost destroyed the makings of the third year's harvest. But I have I enjoyed pruning the trees each year, both in winter and summer, and do this in great hope of a bountiful crop and making a contribution to our Harvest Festival.

I have not gathered fruit by the golden light that harvest moons provide in August and September but these moons have focused my harvest thoughts. I have made an apple store in a corner of the potting shed but it is too easily accessible for mice who selectively eat part of an apple before starting another - an infuriating disturbance to my peace of mind. One year I had a surfeit of apples and although windfalls work wonders in compost heaps they are really too valuable for this. So I bought a heavy-duty Hungarian fruit press and make delicious juice. Its use merits a study in time and motion. First collect apples; well, not quite. First empty the deep freeze to make space for bags of apples; then freeze the apples and allow them to thaw until they become soft and easy to press. Next fill the chamber of the press and turn the handle at the end of the long screw thread above the pressure plate. Juice will soon flow uncontrollably and fill plastic bags to store in the freezer until mid summer. Word has got around that I have a press and it is put to good use locally.

Blackberries *Rubus fruticosus* grow well against a north-facing wall and I have planted two thornless varieties Oregon and Ashton Cross which produce heavy crops in August and September. Oregon has attractive cut leafed foliage and both varieties are little trouble to look after; cutting out the shoots which have fruited, tying in new growth, a thorough manuring in the spring and plenty of water later in the year is all they require.

Gooseberries here also grow well against a north-facing wall but I have no more space. I learnt a lesson from the large old gooseberry bushes; their fruit was delicious but sharp thorns made gathering the berries too prickly a business. So I have planted a line of cordon gooseberries which are easy to prune and harvest so long as I get to them before the blackbirds. The autumn fruiting raspberry *Rubus idoeus* 'Autumn Bliss' is another favourite fruit, all the more so because the blackbirds leave it alone. It is undemanding and after a good dressing of manure bears a heavy crop in

September and October. Only one caution - it spreads vigorously so I have planted my raspberries in a border edged with grass.

A Morello cherry *Prunus avium* is a favourite for a northerly aspect and one grows trained as a fan against the tall vinehouse wall. It requires netting, careful pruning in the Spring and horizontal wires onto which to tie the young shoots. The blossom and the red fruit each make fair pictures. On the other side of the wall, inside the vinehouse, I am trying to grow an apricot *Prunus armeniaca* 'Moorpark' but the vine has priority and its requirement for winter cold does not altogether suit the apricot. As I have often read: a vinehouse should be a vinehouse - just that.

Hazel *Corylus avellana* grows well in the hedgerows around the garden and I relish the nuts so have planted a short allée of ten bushes and am growing more along the meadow boundary; it is an ideal plant to grow as an informal hedge or natural screen. The catkins and tiny red flowers are fascinating and provided squirrels do not take the crop it is nourishing. For centuries local hazels have provided both nuts and stakes and I hope mine will continue to do this. Maintenance is straightforward and involves cutting out a few of the oldest stems in spring, ensuring the cut faces outwards so that water drains away from the crown.

The ancient vines *Vitis* 'Black Hamburgh' and *V.* Muscat of Alexandria, which I believe are as old as the cottage, take pride of place not only amongst my fruit and vegetables but also in the whole garden. I am thrilled to think they have been nurtured here for so long and are now mine to tend. I will always associate the distinctive taste of *V.* 'Muscat of Alexandria' with the garden - perhaps because the grapes were ripe when I first explored it. Since then I have competed with mildew, scald and shanking but can never be certain I will defeat these unwelcome blights. My harvest has improved recently, so much so that I have tried storing bunches in bottles supported at forty degrees in the potting shed rafters. There the bunches hung with the tail end of their stem in water in the neck of a bottle as if they were attached to the vine. However mice soon discovered my grapes and shattered my pride. I have learnt how to prune the rods, thin the bunches, and maintain the correct humidity, and also found clear diagrams and illustrations which help to make caring for these special vines satisfying. But it is their unique harvest that provides such strong incentive to tend them carefully. The vinehouse also provides an unrelated source of both trouble and joy. I become concerned whenever I hear the dull thud of a bird, usually a blackbird, hitting the glass. I do not enjoy replacing shattered panes of glass, nor do I enjoy finding a trapped and frightened bird, but the thrill of the bird's song of freedom and thanks as it flies away compensates for my brief distress.

The quality of my vegetables may not match that of my predecessors Mr Bunney and Mr Haines and I admit to vegetables taking second place to fruit but I enjoy growing vegetables. The potatoes I grew in 1976 won first prize at the village show, although I had to dig up every haulm to find six similar potatoes. On several occasions I have helped children lift potatoes and enjoyed their enthusiasm as they scrabbled to find just one more nestling in the ground. Perhaps, after all, "spud bashing" at school was not such a wasted experience. I never altogether agree that growing potatoes helps to clear ground of invasive weeds, but I know searching for that extra potato will often reveal a tuber or rhizome which comes easily from friable soil.

I grow a useful rather than novel selection of vegetables: onions, runner beans, beetroot, carrots and leeks. Lettuce is, however, my favourite and I plant a succession, Tom Thumb and Little Gem, from February onwards and never tire of them. Rhubarb is another invaluable crop and if I use the forcing-pots I found in the garden I enjoy it from April until August. Vegetables require care and attention and while I find it easy to grow most varieties adequately, extra care of the soil, the seed and planting out make for disproportionately improved results.

So the garden is not only a pleasure garden but also a productive one in which I strive for better results. I am learning all the time - especially that the more you learn the more there is to learn. Meanwhile, I will use my current knowledge while "Doing Gardening".

Chapter 11

"Doing Gardening" - practicalities

My four-year-old nephew did not know of my gardening books, preparations and methods when his sharp eyes noticed me working with favourite tools and called this "Doing Gardening". His expression may be ungrammatical but it describes my practical gardening which I like to think is planned, methodical and single minded. Only in this way can I keep pace with the garden's life and growth, and maintain it in good order.

I have collected a small library of good gardening books belonging to four generations of my family. My great-grandmother owned *Favourite Field Flowers* one hundred and fifty years ago, and my grandmother's name was written beneath her mother's in 1905. This small book contains sensitive Victorian descriptions of cyclamen - sowbread; wild tulips - sweet nurslings of the vernal skies; common ling - *Erica vulgaris*; butterwort; stitchwort and corncockle. My copy of *Sanders Encyclopaedia of Gardening* was my grandfather's; it contains concise plant descriptions and useful methods of cultivation and propagation. He also grew carnations and I enjoy his book *Carnations, Picotees, and the Wild Garden Pinks* - part of the *Country Life Library*. *All About Gardening* was given by my mother to her father and contains his hand-written notes similar to those I add to my books today.

"Doing Gardening" - practicalities

William Robinson's *The English Flower Garden* belonged to Aunt Dorothy who knew and loved her flowers, and after whom I named the orchard. Some of Graham Stuart Thomas' excellent books have been presents from my parents and my brother gave me the Oxford University Press edition of *The Royal Horticultural Society's Dictionary of Gardening*. My own additions to this list are *The Hillier Manual of Trees and Shrubs*, Lucas Phillips' *Small Garden* and Bagenal's *Fruit Growing*. Together all these special books provide a wealth of knowledge about propagation, culture and techniques. Harry Baker's advice about pruning apples and pears, knowledge gained from nearby Sparsholt College and catalogues and newspaper articles all supplement my books and are invaluable for cross reference. I hope that one day a great-nephew or niece may appreciate them and my notebook.

I try not to keep any list of routine garden work: it might be interesting for the record but it would be never-ending, and would remove much of the spontaneity from "Doing Gardening". Sometimes at the busiest of times I succumb to a short list but I laugh at myself when I check it at the end of the day and realise how little I can delete and all I could add. It's a greater pleasure and more satisfying to note in my mind what needs doing and to recall what I have completed; in this way the really important work gets done and I avoid chasing many details. But I do keep lists of plants because although I always think I will remember their names, I don't.

Tools and equipment were not listed amongst the items in the potting shed which Rudyard Kipling described in his poem *The Glory of the Garden* "...the tool and potting shed which are the heart of all, with the cold frames and the hot houses, the dung pits and the tanks, the rollers, carts, and drainpipes with the barrows and the planks"; but tools must have been there, all in their rightful places. I doubt the "...men and 'prentice boys" who are mentioned later in the poem would have shared my obsession for saving time, but by keeping the potting shed tidy I save valuable moments. I find tidiness and good order instil peacefulness and reduce irritation resulting from searches for mislaid equipment - usually found close at hand. I have made a cart for carrying the essential tools I need for "Doing Gardening"; it also carries a bag - a thoughtful present from Aunt Veronica - for rubbish that would otherwise be left in a pile until the end of the day. Collecting it then is a chore and leaving it for collection tomorrow is unsatisfactory.

I find it the greatest pleasure to set aside a whole day for "Doing Gardening", but it is a good test of "love your neighbour" when the rhythm of work is disturbed. Such a gardening day merits planning and self-discipline so as to avoid being distracted by many small tasks that can be done on another occasion, when time is shorter for "Doing Gardening". Maintaining my garden in an orderly manner is an element of my style, and just as plants should be grown well so should compost heaps, paths and gravel be well maintained; this is part of the skill and science of gardening. Visitors often say: "you must have to spend an awful lot of time in your garden"; yes, I do, and find as much satisfaction and happiness in the work as in the result. I am fortunate to enjoy "Doing Gardening".

I start my gardening year in November when I clear up the fallen leaves from among the sturdy young shoots of hellebores and paeonies, and beneath the bright yellow flowers of winter jasmine and heavily scented viburnums. Theirs are not the final flowers of the year, which are those of sedums and nerines, but the first of nature's next year.

Chill damp days, low grey skies, and shortening hours of daylight in November and December restrict gardening. I carefully vary my paths across the lawn and avoid making footprints on frosted grass. It is the time to plant new roses and cut back established ones to reduce the effects of wind, to move or plant young trees and to take hardwood cuttings for the coldframe. In the greenhouse, which I insulate with bubble wrap and which often provides welcome shelter, I tend young plants and may even sow some seeds. In the potting shed I clean the tools and hang them bright and shining in their rightful places. In the vinehouse I clear the fallen leaves and prune the rods before the sap begins to rise, and out of doors I protect

"Doing Gardening" - practicalities

treasured tender plants. On the dampest and greyest days I turn mechanic and service machinery. Mowers, the strimmer and the leaf vacuum are tireless workhorses that respond to good maintenance. When eventually darkness and dampness make time spent outdoors unproductive it is the time to shut the greenhouse, close the lights over the frame, remove muddy boots and enjoy the cheerful warmth of the cottage. Then there's time to read and, immersed in tantalising catalogues, "...perchance to dream".

The effects of cold and damp in mid-January can be very damaging, but seldom in recent years have I needed to brush snow and ice off trees and shrubs. I try to keep the birdbaths free of ice and maintain the air hole through ice on the pond. I put out food for the birds and am always astonished by how quickly they discover it and spread their news around the garden and beyond. I check tree stakes and tie back shoots of climbers trained against the walls. I look out for invasive ivy spreading over walls and remove it there and then - despite it being the emblem of friendship. Cleanliness and hygiene around fruit trees and bushes, and a spray of tar oil winter wash are other forms of maintenance that will pay dividends later. Apples and pears need winter pruning, particularly espalier and cordon trees, but in moderation so as to avoid excessive new growth. Compost heaps benefit greatly from attention and I turn them; this is wonderfully warming but hard work, yet worth the effort for an immediate well managed appearance in the garden, and valuable compost next year. Not least at this time of year I enjoy the company of a spirited robin which, in the shadow of my work, dares to seek a worm.

Fine spring days in February remind me of the week early in February 1982 when I started to remake the walled garden. Now is the time to heal winter's wounds, take precautions against pests, and maintain seats, fences and gutters; this work completed I am ready to join nature's uprising and to begin pruning shrubs which flowered in the second half of last year. I know February is when some clematis will need to be cut back as growth breaks from nodes along the old stems, but I always refer to a good guide.

Even so I have to exercise some judgement when the advice is "...pruning optional"; even more so when it is "...none" and quite obviously the rampageous plant I am studying requires attention. I feed and water clematis regularly from now on and they respond magnificently. Every year I resolve to pay more attention to separating their vigorous stems and tying them in carefully, but all too quickly the plants take charge and grow as they wish. Pruning is a most satisfactory task at this time of year because one is often shaping a plant for the future as opposed to just cutting it back. I am always amazed how the effects of appropriate pruning, sometimes by frost, rejuvenates mature shrubs. As in all gardening work weather conditions are critical and I try not to prune too early, particularly grey leafed plants - santolina, lavender and artemisia; but rubus, cornus, buddleia, viburnum and hypericum all respond well to pruning now. I also wash the white trunks of the silver birch *Betula utilis* var. *jacquemontii*. The higher I reach up the trees the more difficult it becomes to avoid warm soapy water running down inside my shirtsleeves, but the trees seem refreshed for having the winter's algae removed. Towards the end of the month I can't resist sowing seeds and continue to care for these during March - one of the busiest months of the gardening year.

Perhaps it is because I so enjoy working in my garden that the work expands to fill the time available. For whatever reason the days are never long enough and there is much to do. March weather is varied and unpredictable - warm sunny days, cold nights, wind, rain, sleet and snow all feature. I try not to be deceived into thinking spring has arrived early and resist gardening as if it had. Surrounded by snowdrops, aconites, daffodils and early spring blossom I enjoy gardening - sometimes all day. I load the trolley with hand tools, string, a kneeler and a pair of gloves, and to have larger tools ready to hand. I dislike wearing gloves because they make for clumsy hands and deny me the feel of plants and the soil, but they are necessary amongst the spines and prickles of roses, berberis, and thorns. I also dislike gardening in Wellington boots - I won't - and wear leather boots, which breathe.

March is when to clear borders of winter debris, divide herbaceous perennials, and to tend plants as they start their spring growth. It is time also to attack weeds - a concerted assault saves endless weeding later on - how true it is "...one year's seed is seven year's weed". During the winter Jack Frost and worms will break down and draw into the soil the manure I spread in the autumn, and during a dry spell I will complete the process and fork over the soil making it light and friable. There are roses to prune, the vine to tie up and the first tasks in the routine of lawncare. The days are growing longer which is helpful as I work to keep pace with spring's growth. "Doing Gardening" begins to take on a new purpose with the prospect of the garden being "Open to the Public" next month, and getting it in good order now leads to pleasure in maintaining it throughout the year.

Everything opens in April (Latin aperire = to open); the earth releases new life, the sky releases showers, and as gardeners we shed our cocoon of winter clothing. Our sense of freedom asserts itself and suddenly winter is past. It becomes even more important to do one thing at a time. Seedlings in the greenhouse need care and I pot on older plants that continue to require frost protection, yet I may apply shade protection to the glass. I watch tender young growth and try to protect it when frost is forecast. One of the few painful aspects of gardening is facing up to spring frost damage which can so suddenly lay waste to all success with earlier precautions. In my garden I never feel annoyed with nature but I do find Jack Frost malevolent. On a more hopeful note a feed for roses will induce strong and repeated blooms, and newly planted shrubs and trees will benefit greatly from generous watering. I hoe the earth around the bases of the young trees in the meadow and keep them clear of hungry weeds. I deadhead bulbs as their blooms fade and if I find myself on top of my work I spray the bulbs' foliage. This is such an easy task with a modern feeder attached to a hose that I often continue and feed all the hedges and plants through their foliage. So much for doing one task at a time. But as a bonus from feeding everything I have an opportunity to take stock of what else needs doing - in particular whether the grey leafed plants are ready for pruning. When new growth breaks strongly from the base of their stems then they should be pruned.

May is the month for hoeing, transplanting and tending spring growth; all to be enjoyed during lengthening days and the overwhelming beauty of the season. "Doing Gardening" before breakfast at this time of year is my idea of heaven. A visitor once asked me (warning me the question would be a very personal one) if I ever ate breakfast in my garden. "Yes" I replied, but I failed to say it tastes better having gardened for an hour beforehand. Generous mulching when the soil is damp and warm saves time later on and, just as a day's assistance in the garden makes my week eight days long, so I hope an improved watering system with adequate taps and seephose will make it even longer. I use the trolley and its bank of tools regularly, sometimes going round the whole garden in one day - weeding, hoeing, tying, thinning, staking, deadheading and noticing what needs to be done - all the time absorbing the atmosphere of spring. It never seems there is a lot to do so long as I feel ahead, or at least abreast, of the garden's growth. Every day there is something new to enjoy and encouragement from seeing the results of earlier work.

"Doing Gardening" in June when the foliage of trees and hedges is bright green, the swallows are flying high and the days seem endless, is an encore of May's heaven. I notice gaps in the borders but am wary because many plants will yet make a great deal of growth and the gaps will soon be filled. I feel bad if later in the year I notice plants smothering each other with their summer growth - sometimes because of my earlier anxiety that every space should be filled. Tulips concern me at this time of year - to lift or not? Whenever I have lifted them I have seldom been successful with the bulbs another year; but left in a border amongst roses they respond to a hefty mulch of manure and most continue to give a brilliant display. Amongst all else to care for now is the lawn, its edges and other grass throughout the garden. I find this work rewarding and appreciate how fortunate I am to regard it in this way. A healthy lawn, edged with care, sets off the garden and makes faults elsewhere less obvious, but if I allow the grass to become unkempt the whole garden looks neglected. However, after an hour or so of exercise behind an efficient mower good order can easily be restored. Even more so after I trim the privet, thorn and evergreen oak hedges. I cut the box hedges at the end of this month - after the first flush of growth - so as to allow time for subsequent growth to harden before winter frosts. The box hedges respond well and the result of cutting them adds a characteristic fragrance to the garden. On a damp, misty yet warm June evening trachelospermum, jasmine, roses, stocks, sweet peas and broom also fill the air with their unique scents.

Perennials should be deadheaded now if they are to give of their best, many if cut back will flower again, and michaelmas daisies if 'tipped' will not grow as tall as if left untouched. Pests find plenty to enjoy and disfigure at this time of year, but idleness, shortage of time, and ecology all make me averse to using chemicals as pesticides. I prefer nature to take her course and I particularly enjoy unfurling a diseased leaf to find a ladybird hunting aphids. Rabbits and cats vie with wind and Jack Frost as my principal garden enemies Cats do, however, hunt rabbits which live beyond my boundary, but this credit hardly balances their cruelty towards birds. Rabbits seldom get into the walled garden but in the meadow they enjoy breaking young shoots and ring barking trees so I protect all I can. I could do without these invaders and have no sympathy for them when those I startle dash fearfully for safety beyond my boundary.

High summer is a wonderful time to be "Doing Gardening". I keep a pair of secateurs indoors and most mornings before breakfast make a round of the garden, deadheading roses by cutting away not just the old bloom but also a length of stem. It's when to notice greenfly and to spray infested plants, preferably early or late in the day. If I notice blackspot then my earlier precautions against this unsightly disease have failed and the best I can do is to prevent the spores residing in the soil and to remove infected leaves. I compare gardening in July, when nature is at full power and the garden enthrals me, to driving a Rolls Royce motor car with a strong silent engine, a substantial chassis and elegant coachwork painted with great depth of colour. The garden in its turn feels strong and sweet, has plenty in reserve and its colour is full and deep.

The foliage of the bulbs in the meadow is ready for cutting together with the long grass. If I tackle all this by degrees my own machinery can cope. Each year in the meadow moles from beyond my boundary tunnel and excavate mounds of fine soil. I would let them continue undisturbed except that the ground looks uncared for and molehills look unsightly; but I don't want to kill them so instead of trapping I soak rags in Renardine, a very pungent liquid, and place these in the runs - the moles soon turn away.

I have propagated many young plants from softwood cuttings at this time of year. Mist and a warm base have increased my success rate since early days when I enclosed cuttings in transparent bags. Each year I learn more about using the mist propagator and how to grow on the plants which root so readily. I use composted bark and Perlite as a propagating medium - solely to support the cuttings - and within weeks most will have rooted; I then pot them on into nutritious compost and give them sufficient light, water and drainage. While in the mood for propagating I feel encouraged to sow wallflower and foxglove seeds for next year.

The borders receive careful attention now. If I staked carefully at the end of May the hazel stakes will be unnoticeable, but useful when tying in new growth. Watering and deadheading continue to be important and also some judicious gap filling with replacement plants. Whenever I set off from the potting shed for the herbaceous borders I gather all I need. The borders are far from the shed and returning to collect whatever I have forgotten is a wretched waste of time. Towards the end of this month I cut the hornbeam and beech hedges; this does not take long and improves the appearance of the garden immensely. I reach the high hedges using a ladder across the top of which I tie a plank to spread the load against the hedge. So July is a full month, but not overfull, and I make time to visit other gardens and study the planting.

August is a month to spend at home - far from the madding crowd. There is something constant and interminable about summer days in August when morning noon and night - day after day - run together into one glorious stretch of time. A feeling inherited perhaps from long school summer holidays. I hope the young families who over the years have lived next door at Itchen Gate have experienced similar feelings. One family was very musical and practised together on their various instruments. Their music filled the garden and encouraged me to relax and enjoy the place all the more, sometimes in the pond garden with the dancing dragon and damselflies. When the music stopped there was always gardening to be done.

Trimming the yew hedges is a priority task in early August. A bonus from yew hedging is the use of the fresh young clippings for making a drug which is helping the fight against breast cancer. The hedges here yield 140 kilograms of clippings which I store and turn over regularly in the garage until within a week they are loaded into bags, weighed and taken away to Yorkshire. A substance - Taxol - is then extracted from the yew to make the drug Taxotere. But 1,000 kilograms of clippings are needed to make just 200 grams of this valuable drug. In many places yew is now being grown commercially for Taxol and I sometimes think I might do the same in the top section of the meadow, perhaps as a maze. But this is probably one of those good "good ideas" I should not pursue.

I enjoy walking in the garden during a summer's evening as the light begins to fade and the colours intensify. I notice but make only a subconscious list of what needs to be done - wisteria to be pruned, penstemon cuttings to be struck, lavender flowers to be dried and fruit to be harvested. At this time of year it does not really matter whether the blackberries are picked tomorrow or another day because I know such work will not be forgotten.

At the end of the month the moon rises quickly like a bouncing ball through the trees to the east and seems to hang above the garden. This is the time to walk round again, sit on every seat and, without the distraction of colour or noticing whatever needs doing, absorb myself in the atmosphere of the place. An atmosphere similar, but on a smaller scale, to that which T E Lawrence found in the desert, and described in *The Seven Pillars of Wisdom*: "The abstraction of the desert landscape cleansed me, and rendered my mind vacant with its superfluous greatness: a greatness achieved not by the addition of thought to its emptiness, but by its subtraction. In the weakness of earth's life was mirrored the strength of heaven, so vast, so beautiful, so strong". In my garden I can find similar strength and peace.

The heady days of August are a foretaste of September - one of the most beautiful months of the year when days shorten rapidly and evenings begin to feel cool. But the colours are strong and growing stronger, there is a harvest of fruit to be gathered, plants to be cared for and work on the lawns. The weather is usually perfect for "Doing Gardening" - energetically. Whenever and wherever possible I try to get ahead of the garden because all too soon October will arrive with much to be done to the borders. It is time to turn my hands and eyes to the nursery and greenhouse where young plants need care - thinning, weeding, and repotting - and to prepare hardwood cuttings. Bulbs ordered in the summer may arrive and require planting and herbaceous cuttings should be struck. At this time of year I never deny myself the pleasure of picking and enjoying an apple before breakfast and, later in the day, enjoying grapes from the vine. September is the month to fit in a holiday although I never want to leave the garden for long and have even returned early; but a break is good and I come back, often with Welsh inspiration, to garden intensively and complete the year with October's work.

October is a month of mixed emotions and activity - clearing up and cutting back summer's abundant growth, combined with planting out and looking forward to spring. Much of the pleasure of gardening is anticipation; border by border I go through the garden and gather up compostable rubbish. It seems cruel to cut down cosmos and other summer annuals while they are in bloom but their space is needed for wallflowers, forget-me-nots and tulips. These in their turn will make way for more cosmos and annuals. I look forward to the day I own a shredder and speed up compost making, but for the present layers of herbaceous material go between layers of soil or manure. After several turnings and the work of earthworms the compost heaps will become dark piles. I maintain heaps in corners of the garden and near each I build others. In a tank by the potting shed I use fresh comfrey leaves to make a brew of liquid manure which, because it smells so strongly, I think must be good.

Amongst my machinery I have a leaf vacuum machine but in the darkest and dampest corners I find working on hands and knees more efficient and remember Kipling's words "...half a proper gardener's work is done upon his knees". I am glad to get close to my work because in corners amongst sodden debris I often disturb frogs which thought they had made themselves a home for the winter. They give me a sideways glance, as much as to say "must you" before they grope their way lethargically to safety and a new hideaway. It is also good to be on hands and knees because not only is it the most comfortable position in which to collect rubbish from the ground, but it is also the best position from which to take a close look at what's happening - a look I share yet again with that bright robin seeking a worm. But it's not "eyes down and look in" all the time and I find myself looking up at swans or geese which whisper through the air, or at the autumn colours on the trees.

I reckon the year comes to an end as the first frosts blacken the dahlias' foliage. That is when to lift the tubers, upend them and to store them for the winter. "Doing Gardening" is a fulfilling and happy recreation - all the more so when I can look back on a year's productive work and forward with hope.

Chapter 12

Going Public - added value

GARDEN OPEN The National Gardens Scheme

"Please will you open your garden to the public for the National Gardens Scheme - just once or perhaps twice a year?" A request similar to asking someone to join a committee "... a meeting just once a quarter". Of course it turns out not to be not at all like that. Garden opening proves the rule "you get out of it as much as you put in"; it has been a thrill which has led to much else. "Do you ever talk about your garden?" "Do you ever have visits by groups?" "I know of someone who..." "Do you know that...?" "Would you ever come and give me some advice?" I was anxious preparing for the first opening, but that's only right. I would be inviting the public to pay to visit my garden; they would expect to see a good garden and I would want it to look its best. I dread the occasion I cannot achieve this, just as I also dread forgetting a group is planned to visit. I wonder how I'll react; perhaps I'll be away which will make matters worse.

Of course I am pleased to have my garden in the 'Yellow Book' - that best selling encyclopaedia *Gardens Open for Charity*. In early September efficiently compiled papers arrive, inviting commitment to open the following year. These papers include questions which if answered incorrectly will lead to disappointment for visitors, eg plants for sale/not for sale, teas or tea (the latter means tea and biscuits only) and considerable embarrassment. Assistance, parking, notices, tables for tea and plants, and a welcome all need to be planned. Visitors do not want to be bombarded with extras, but they do enjoy a plant stall and appreciate sitting down with at least a cup of tea. Signs to the garden are essential. That large yellow sign 'Garden Open' is the most important and I felt I really had arrived - but only that - when I was given my own. I will have to open for twenty-one years for my silver trowel.

Before one of my earliest openings on a St George's Day a friend said he would come if I would fly St George's Cross. The thought of buying a flagpole went against the grain so I asked a builder to lend me a scaffold pole. "Yes alright, you look like the sort of person who will bring it back" he replied. I returned later without the pole to thank him for his loan but he spoke first: "You want to keep it, don't you". So the pole now stands beside the potting shed in a corner of the garden where it can be seen from everywhere; it has become an important unifying feature in my design. I fly St George's Cross on high days and holidays and the Union flag on other specific days. St George's Cross was given to me by Elizabeth Halliday who had given it to the church overlooking her garden at Llandovery in south Wales; but whereas it did not fly acceptably in Wales it flies proudly here. Whatever the flag it provides visitors with a unique memory of my garden.

I give visitors a leaflet about the garden as part of their welcome. It includes answers to some of the most usual questions, but there is no substitute for answering these personally. Friends say I am too honest with my answers and that when I have forgotten the name of a plant I could surely think up a more original answer in place of "I don't know, but I'll find out". I remember the Baluch officer in Oman who had been nominated as gardens member for our camp; perhaps I should follow his example. During a tour with him round the barracks I asked the name of one of the few trees. He considered carefully and then replied quickly "Green tree, sir". I have labelled trees and could label more plants, but most labels have a short life and a perverse will of their own, often hiding behind foliage or displaying their reverse.

I dislike missing friends who later say how sorry they were not to see me when they visited and "Were you there?" I am always around but may have been talking to someone else. Such conversations are an enjoyable but tiring part of opening the garden. "Do you ever have time to sit down?" and "how many gardeners do you employ?" are frequent questions to which I try to give original answers. I challenge thoughtful comments such as "There is an atmosphere of peace and space in your garden". "Why?" I ask, and there usually follows a fulfilling appreciation of the design, choice of plants and surroundings.

"Where do we start?" is a question that gives me an opportunity to direct visitors to the terrace where photographs illustrate the different stages of construction, and provide a feeling for the place. Thus prepared visitors are off to a good start and ready for unexpected interest round each corner. There are surprises, nothing alarming like the fountains which drenched unwary visitors who walked in the Italian garden at Villa D'Este, but sufficient to help retain their interest and encourage them to follow what I hope seems a natural route - seeing the garden as I intend it should be seen. But some visitors go their own way and return with refreshing observations and questions. "What part of the garden do you like best?" is my favourite. Without hesitation I reply "Wherever I happen to be working".

I sometimes study visitors and picture their gardens. Occasionally I provoke comment or maybe just stand nearby and listen, either way I learn much. I keep a watchful eye on suspicious visitors, or better still ask inquisitive children to do so, but I learnt too late. One Sunday two unlikely gardeners paid their entrance fee but our eyes never met through their dark glasses. I noticed them walking round in a disinterested way and know they spent some time admiring Hebe. That night she was stolen. I was saddened because I had lost a good ornament, and annoyed because thieves had been in my garden during a summer's night and I had heard nothing.

But another Hebe, although a replacement and standing in concrete, now graces the allée serenely.

National Gardens Scheme openings started in 1926 when most visitors must have travelled by bus and "...alight at Rectory Lane" would have been a helpful instruction. No sooner had I removed this instruction from my directions than an American visitor telephoned to enquire where she should get off the bus. "You must be Mrs Green", I replied. She was taken aback so I explained that only the day before friends had met her after she had travelled by bus to visit their garden. They had got to know her as Mrs Green and perchance were with me when she arrived at Abbey Cottage; so we gave her a cheerful welcome.

Visits by a group merit careful preparation. Where has the group come from? What might any special interests be? Should I give a guided tour or let members explore? Whatever else I always welcome a group and did this for my first coach load of knowledgeable and enthusiastic gardeners in July 1995 - another step in 'going public'. Coaches are a problem; turning, parking, loading and unloading all occupy precious moments. The visitors themselves are always interested and grateful; they have come for no other purpose than to enjoy the garden with friends, and to hear about it. I regret there is seldom long enough to do justice to either them or the garden. I was delighted for one group of visitors when at the start of their visit - mine was the final visit of their holiday - I promised to make it their best; on leaving they assured me it had been. On other occasions it has been rewarding to refer to plants, very correctly, by their botanical names - this, particularly with foreigners, often results in a good rapport.

Younger people who are making a garden of their own and seeking ideas receive my undivided attention, and I hope they take away inspiration similar to that I was given by garden owners twenty years ago. I had always hoped the garden would create interest for them and believed this in itself would make 'going public' worthwhile. Children also get my special attention and it thrills me when they play hide and seek and are cunning enough never to get caught.

Just as I welcome visitors on open days, so I welcome individual visits made by appointment and I am learning fast how best to handle these. I resist "Doing Gardening" as I escort visitors and have long ceased saying "If only you were here last week you would have seen...". I am also learning not to comment on all I personally like and enjoy but rather to exercise restraint and allow visitors to judge for themselves, and comment as they wish; this often leads to thoughtful opinions and discussion. I grow quickly to like most visitors, but there are some who I hope never notice if I encourage them not to dally. They seem to have forgotten to shut their own garden gates, and are usually reluctant to want to leave mine. I sometimes say to more favoured guests what the monks at St Catherine's Monastery in the Sinai said when they showed me their library: "99% of our visitors do not visit our library", but here I say: "Only 1% of my guests see inside the potting shed".

I enjoyed six months of good visits when Gill and Jim Thomas made gardening videos here together with their horticultural experts and film crews. The latter respected the garden, but I needed to interrupt their initial enthusiasm for their photography to explain the garden to them. Cameramen may have left footprints as evidence of their ambition to get the best shot possible, and the sound team may have expected silence from everything except their subject, but I enjoyed their professionalism. A few minutes on BBC2 Gardeners World *The Great British Gardening Show* gave my garden an enormous fillip in 1994. This was, for a moment, 'going public' in a big way and now, when travelling through the country, I am thrilled to think that pictures of my garden were transmitted everywhere. That the garden has been included in the Channel 4 series *The 20th Century Garden* is another fillip and an occasion when I hope to give due credit to the people and places which have influenced my garden. Having the garden listed in garden books and guides is also exciting especially when I see

'Abbey Cottage' printed on a map; and not only in books in this country but also in Sweden and Japan.

My most exhilarating visitors have been Lord Coggan and his wife. We all featured in the Gardener's World television programme, they in their allotment beside Winchester Cathedral. There Lord Coggan described himself as the "under gardener" to his wife and declared with awful simplicity "...the only way to get rid of a thistle is to pull it up by the roots". Their recognition of the peace, space and beauty of the plants and flowers here thrilled me. Lord Coggan's appreciation of gardens is profound. In his book *A Voice from the Cross* he wrote of paradise: " 'In Paradise'. The word is Persian and means a garden, a park, an enclosure. People have striven hard to find pictures which convey the idea of a blissful afterlife. The writer of Revelation depicted the new heaven as a city of pure gold, bright as clear glass, its foundations adorned with precious stones of every kind (Revelation 21.18-21). That imagery will, no doubt, help some, but I for one find the horticultural more helpful than the architectural. A park or garden speaks of serenity and beauty, and it speaks of ongoing activity, of gardeners in co-operation with the creator - there is little beauty in a park where no work is done. Heaven thought of in these terms speaks of growth, development, creativity, of creatures and creator happy in collusion." I humbly echo Lord Coggan's description and find my garden offers unlimited opportunities for growth, development and creativity - all amidst the life and energy of so many and varied creatures which seem happy to be here.

Although the garden is mine, much that I do is related to it being open to the public in a week, a month, or in six months' time, and I want it to be considered a garden worth visiting. This has become even more important since I started giving illustrated talks during which in forty-five minutes I show my audience a year's worth of my best pictures. I encourage them to visit the garden and therefore want to match their expectations. These talks have taken my garden to village halls throughout Hampshire and to

Going Public - added value

varied audiences, each with its individual character but similar nature, whether garden club, horticultural society or Women's Institute. Village halls also have unique character and similarities. They seem desolate when I arrive before the keyholder but soon become a hive of activity and light when people assemble and switch on wall heaters, drag folding chairs and tables from awkward cupboards, and arrange the hall "as if it could never have been any other way". For a moment I may feel alone in the sociable crowd, while raffles are organised, business conducted and plants assembled for the monthly competition. However I have never experienced anything but the warmest of welcomes which have quickly dispelled any loneliness. When the lights go out I make my garden come alive and try to include at least one picture so as to be able to say: "today this plant was at its best". There are different ways of gauging the success of a talk, but if the audience asks to arrange a visit to my garden and they subsequently enjoy it, that is surely the best indication.

That's something about 'going public'.

Afterword

There, then, is the story of my garden - up to date insofar as it will ever be - and written by an amateur with all the advantages and disadvantages my lack of horticultural training generates. My thoughts about the garden and working in it have been in anticipation of creating an exceptional one; a task which has fused my efforts with my passion, and provided opportunities for exercising talents and creativity. Ever since I found Abbey Cottage the development and enjoyment of the place has, in Vita Sackville-West's words, provided "...that ardour which lit the whole".

I recently discovered a discreet plaque in a private garden in Northumberland. The inscription on it read "As a humble mark of gratitude for happiness passed". The Winchester Cathedral stonemasons have carved an identical inscription on a plaque, and added the date MDCCCCIC. It marks the close of the 20th century at Abbey Cottage and many years of gardening creativity and good friendships. The inscription would have been too long and its message divided had I added "...and hope for the future"; but that's the prospect.

Appendix

Some design principles:
"Successful garden design results in a garden that could be in no other way."
(Dame Sylvia Crowe).

Style
- choose a design which is definite and which has a strong framework; this will help to create the character of the garden.
- incorporate and make use of existing features, both those within and outside your boundary.
- make an uncluttered approach to the garden so that the latter becomes a striking surprise.
- take ideas from other places and other gardens, but adapt them so that your garden is truly your own, and in your own style.
- finishing touches, which often help to make the garden labour saving, will make your own mark on the garden and help create unity in the design.
- good design is simple design.
- care and maintenance are essential for a beautiful garden.

Unity
- plan the garden as a whole, and with singleness of thought and purpose.
- unite and link the house and the garden - views, vistas, doors, windows, paving.
- avoid too many different and ill digested features.
- make the garden compatible and in keeping with the surroundings.
- use local materials but not too great a variety of them.
- focal points help to create vistas and concentrate one's gaze; do not spoil vistas by creating conflicting lateral interests.

- hedges of one species; the same colour on all painted woodwork; and the way in which separate areas are joined together all contribute to unity.
- the over-arching canopy of a tree can help to unite all beneath it.
- create glimpses of what is to come next as one moves through the garden.

Space Division
- divide the area so that the complete garden is not seen at one view.
- plant hedges for division, height, and an unbroken background (unity); be patient while hedges grow - there is much interest and pleasure in growing a hedge well, and even yew can grow one foot a year.
- make full use of corners to create interest and help reduce labour (eg awkward grass areas to cut).
- if the site allows, create different levels; these will contribute enormously to interest and variety in the garden.

Scale
- correct proportion leads to harmony and a peaceful atmosphere.
- ornaments and features are more often too small rather than too large.
- the width of borders, paths, steps and paving, and the height of features (ornaments and fountains) all contribute to scale and proportion.
- a mistake in small gardens is to scale down too much.
- good proportion: breadth to length (Golden Section); open space to planted area; horizontal to vertical.

Plants and Colour
- contrast the planting in different areas; do not have the same planting patterns recurring at every turn; be generous with your planting, and make full use of annuals.
- grow the plants you like in positions they like.
- pleasure from colours and plant associations derives from your taste (beauty is in the eye of the beholder); in my garden blue, grey, pink, white,

light green and pale colours are together, leaving yellow, brown, red and deep green together elsewhere. I use groups of strong coloured plants to strengthen my design. Texture and foliage help to create and complete the picture.

- understand pruning - when, where, and why.

Bibliography

Bagenal, N B. *Fruit Growing*, (Ward Lock) 1939

Coggan, Donald. *The Voice from the Cross*, (Triangle) 1993

Cook, E T. (editor) *Carnations, Picotees, and the Wild Garden Pinks*, (Country Life and George Newnes) 1905

Cowley, Abraham. *The Wish*, 1647

Crowe, Sylvia. *Garden Design*, (Country Life) 1958

Grey, Edward. *Fly Fishing*, (J M Dent) 1907

Grey of Falloden. *The Charm of Birds*, (Hodder and Stoughton) 1927

Housman, A E. *A Shropshire Lad*, 1896

Jekyll, Gertrude. *Home and Garden*, (Longman and Green) 1900

Kingsley, Charles. *The Water Babies*, (J M Dent) 1957

Kipling, Rudyard. *The Glory of the Garden*, 1912

Lawrence, T E. *The Seven Pillars of Wisdom*, (Jonathan Cape) 1941

Lucas Phillips, C E. *The Small Garden*, (William Heinemann) 1952

Page, Russell. *The Education of a Gardener*, (Collins) 1962

Pevsner, Nikolaus, and David Lloyd. *The Buildings of England*, (Penguin Books Ltd) 1967

Robinson, W. *The English Flower Garden*, (Murray) 1903

Sanders, T W. *The Encyclopaedia of Gardening*, (Collingridge) 14th Edition, circa 1913

Hillier Manual of Trees and Shrubs, (Redwood Press) 1991

Royal Horticultural Society, Dictionary of Gardening, (Oxford University Press) 1974

Favourite Field Flowers, circa 1850, author unknown

All About Gardening, (Ward Lock), circa 1930, author unknown

Index

A

Abelia x *grandiflora,* 74
Abeliophyllum dissectum, 66
Acanthus mollis, 70
Acer griseum, 55
Actinidia kolomikta, 76
Aesculus indica, 57
  A. parviflora, 57
Aegopodium podagraria 'Variegatum', 73
Ajuga reptans, 74
Alchemilla mollis, 67
allée, 23, 35, 45, 51, 68
Allium nigrum, 68
Aloysia triphylla, 67
Althaea rosea, 68
Amelanchier canadensis, 56
Anaphalis triplivernis, 70
Anemone blanda, 70
  A. x *hybrida* 'Honorine Joubert', 77
  A. seemanii, 67
Apples
  Bramley, 35, 53, 87
  Cox's Orange Pippin, 53, 88
  Discovery, 89
  Lady Henniker, 32, 35, 53, 68, 88
  Tydeman's Late Orange, 89
  Washington, 31, 52, 65, 88
Arabis fernandi-coburgii, 68
Artemisia 'Powis Castle', 76
Asplenium scolopendrium, 73
Aster novae-angliae, 70
Aubrieta spp, 65

B

Bergenia cordifolia, 66
Betula pendula 'Dalecarlica', 58
  B. utilis var. *jacquemontii,* 58
box seat, 23, 50

Brunnera macrophylla, 73
Buddleia fallowiana 'Lochinch', 70
Bunney, William, 26, 31, 89, 92
bus shelter, 45, 56
Buxus sempervirens 'Aureovariegata', 50
  B. sempervirens 'Handsworthiness', 50
  B. sempervirens 'Suffruticosa', 49

C

Castlewellan, 56
Ceanothus 'Autumnal Blue', 69
  C. 'Puget's Blue', 76
Caltha palustris, 69, 84
Carex riparia, 74
Carpinus betulus, 52
Caryopteris x *clandonensis* 'Heavenly Blue', 38
Catalpa bignionoides 'Aurea', 58
Cedrus deodara 'Aurea', 58
Ceratostigma griffithii, 69
  C. willmottianum, 69
Chaenomeles speciosa 'Nivalis' 76
Chimonanthus praecox, 66
Choysia ternata, 65
Cistus x *corbariensis,* 74
Cladrastis lutea, 59
  C. sinensis, 58
Clematis 'Alba Luxurians', 76
  C. armandii, 76
  C. cirrhosa 'Balearica', 66
  C. 'Jackmanii', 73
  C. 'Marie Boisselot', 73
  C. 'Nelly Moser', 73
  C. 'Polish Spirit', 73
  C. 'Lord Nevill', 66
  C. macropetala 'Markham's Pink', 73
  C. orientalis 'Bill Mackenzie', 65

C. rehderiana, 76
C. viticella, 69
Cleome spinosa, 68
Coggan, Donald, 112
Convallaria majalis, 65
Cornus alba 'Elegantissima', 65, 70
  C. alba 'Spaethii', 73
  C. alternifolia 'Argentea', 69
  C. contraversa 'Eddie's White Wonder', 74
Coronilla glauca, 76
Cortaderia 'Pumila', 74
Corydalis lutea, 67
Corylus avellana, 91
Cotinus coggyria, 74
Cotoneaster horizontalis, 67
  C. horizontalis 'Variegatus', 73
Crataegus prunifolia, 59
Crinum x powellii, 71
Crocus chrysanthus 'Cream Beauty', 65
Crowe, Sylvia, 18, 20, 23, 117
Cyclamen coum, 68
Cynoglossum amabile 'Firmament', 68
Cytisus battandieri, 71

D

Dahlia 'Bishop of Llandaff', 68
Daphne mezereum alba, 66
  D. odora, 74
design principles, 20, 21, 117
Dianthus 'Mrs Sinkins', 65, 68
Dicentra exima 'Alba', 67
Dorycnium hirsutum, 70

E

Elaeagnus angustifolia, 74
  E. ebbingei, 75
Elodea canadensis, 85
Epimedium pinnatum colchium, 66
E. pubigerum, 66
E. x rubrum, 66
Erica carnea, 65
Erigeron karvinskiansus, 65, 67
Erisymum alpinum, 76
  E. linifolium, 76
Euchryphia x nymansiensis 'Nymansay', 68
Euonymous alatus, 74
  E. fortunei 'Silver Pillar', 72
  E. fortunei 'Silver Queen', 68
Euphorbia characias, 70
  E. myrsinites, 74
  E. polychroma, 67
Exochorda macrantha, 74

F

Fagus sylvatica, 51
  F. sylvatica 'Purple Fountain', 59
  F. sylvatica var. *heterophylla* 'Asplenifolia', 59
Felicia echinata, 66
Festuca glauca, 74
Fraxinus excelsior 'Jaspidea', 59
Fremontodendron californicum, 75
Fritillaria meleagris, 80
Fuchsia triphylla, 65

G

Galanthus nivalis, 65
Geranium cinereum, 67
  G. dalmaticum, 67
  G. procurrens, 76
  G. subcaulescens, 65
Ginkgo biloba, 59
Golden Section, 21, 36, 83, 118
grass seed, 'Manhattan', 78
Grey, Edward of Falloden, 27, 41
Ground elder see *Aegopodium podagraria* 'Variegatum'

H

Hebe armstrongii, 70
Helianthemum nummularium, 74
　H. nummularium 'Wisley Primrose', 65
Helleborus niger, 67
　H. orientalis, 65
Hemerocallis minor, 76
　H. multiflora, 76
Hibiscus syriacus, 74
Hosta sieboldii, 67
Hyacinthoides hispanica 'Alba', 65
Hydrangea 'Lanarth White', 66
　H. ' Mme Emile Mouillère', 67
Hypericum calycinum, 66

I

Ilex aquifolium 'Argentea Marginata Pendula', 60
Ipheion uniflorum, 76
Iris laevigata, 76
　I. pseudocorus, 70
　I. stylosa, 65
Itea ilicifolia, 66

J

Jenkyn Place, 23, 51, 58, 61, 74
Juglans regia, 60
Juniperus chinensis 'Aurea', 56, 70
　J. communis 'Hibernica', 56

K

Koelreuteria paniculata, 57
Kolkwitzia amabilis, 74

L

Lamium maculatum, 73
Lathyrus chloranthus, 76
　L. sativus, 76
Lavandula angustifolia, 56, 70

Ligustrum ovalifolium, 74
Lilium candidum, 67
Limnanthes douglassii, 74
Liquidambar stryaciflua, 57
Lobelia cardinalis, 69
Lonicera fragrantissima, 71
　L. nitida 'Baggesen's Gold', 65
　L. periclymenum 'Serotina', 74
　L. periclymenum 'Graham Stuart Thomas', 75

M

Mahonia aquifolium, 67
　M. x media 'Lionel Fortescue', 65
Magnolia grandiflora 'Exmouth', 60
　M. x loebneri 'Merrill', 55, 70
Malus tschonoskii, 55
Matteuccia struthiopteris, 73
Miscanthus sinensis 'Variegatus', 69
Molinia caerulea, 74
Morus nigra, 57
Myosotis palustris, 84
Myrtus communis, 65
　M. communis 'Microphylla Variegata', 70

N

Narcissus 'Jack Snipe', 76
　N. 'Jenny', 76
　N. 'Peeping Tom', 80
　N. poeticus var. *recurvus*, 80
National Gardens Scheme, 107, 110
National Trust, 23
Nerine bowdenii, 67, 76
Nepeta x fassenii, 68, 76
Nymphae 'Escarboucle', 70, 83
　N. 'Rose Arey', 70, 83

O

Oman, Sultanate of, 17, 24, 38, 40, 42, 68

Omphalodes cappadocica, 73
   O. cappadocica 'Starry Eyes', 70
Ostrya carpinifolia, 60

P

Paeonia mlokosewitschii, 70
   P. officinalis, 70
Page, Russell, 18, 20, 63
paint, on woodwork, 23
Pears
  Beurre de Rance, 31
  Nouveau Poiteau, 88
  Comice, 88
  Concorde, 88
Persicaria affine, 65, 67, 73
Philadelphus 'Belle Etoile', 74
Pilgrim's Way, 79
Pittisporum garnettii, 79
Polygonatum odoratum, 67
pond, 36, 69, 83
Potentilla fruticosa 'Abbotswood', 67, 70
Primula spp, 65
Prunus 'Accolade', 61
   P. armeniaca 'Moor Park', 91
   P. avium 'Plena', 61
   P. sargentii, 61
   P. spinosa, 52
   P. subhirtella, 54
Punica granatum, 76
Pyracantha 'Sparkler', 72
Pyrus nivalis, 55
   P. salicifolia, 55

Q

Quercus ilex, 51

R

Ribes sanguineum 'Tydeman's White', 66
   R. speciosum, 72
Rosa 'Anne of Gerstein', 75

R. 'Anthea Fortescue', 67
R. 'Beautiful Britain', 36, 69
R. 'Californica Plena', 75
R. 'Céline Forrestier', 68
R. 'Danse du Feu', 73
R. 'Golden Showers', 76
R. 'Iceberg', 76
R. 'Kathleen Harrop', 68
R. 'Madame Alfred Carrière', 73
R. 'Margaret Merrill', 67
R. 'Mermaid', 73
R. 'Nathalie Nypels', 69, 71
R. 'New Dawn', 73
R. 'Parkdirektor Riggers', 67
R. 'Phyllis Bide', 71
R. *pomifera*, 75
R. 'Pompon de Paris', 69
R. *rubrifolia*, 70
R. *rugosa* 'Alba', 75
R. 'St Swithun', 74
R. 'Sultan Qaboos', 68
R. 'Winchester Cathedral', 74
R. *xanthina* 'Canary Bird', 75
R. 'Zepherine Drouhin', 67
Rosmarinus officinalis, 65
Rubus cockburnianus, 70
   R. fruticosus, 90
   R. idoeus, 90

S

Salvia patens, 68
St Catherine's Monastery, 111
St George's Cross, 108
Sarcococca confusa, 66
Saxifraga × urbium 'London Pride', 67
Schizophragma hydrangeoides, 66
Sedum 'Autumn Joy', 70
Silene uniflora, 65
Sisyrynchium 'Californian Skies', 67
Sorbus thibetica 'John Mitchell', 57
   S. vilmorinii, 54

Spiraea japonica 'Goldflame', 70
steps, 21, 35, 36, 41, 67, 118
summer wildflowers, 79
Symphytum grandiflorum, 65
Stipa gigantica, 67
Syringa vulgaris 'Madame Lemoine', 74

T

Tanacetum herderi, 65
Taxol, 104
Taxotere, 104
Taxus baccata, 50, 51
  T. baccata 'Fastigiata', 56
television,
  BBC 2 'Gardener's World', 111
  Channel 4 'The 20th Century Garden', 111
Tetradium danielli, 61
Teuchrium fruticans, 75
Thalmocalamnus spathiflora, 73
Thymus 'Doone Valley', 65
Tiarella cordifolia, 73, 74
Tilia henryana, 61
Tolmeia menziesii, 66
Trachelospermum asiaticum, 66, 76
Tulipa 'Appledoorn', 67
  T. 'Gordon Cooper', 69
Typha latifolia, 84

V

Veronica gentianoides, 67
  V. peduncularis, 70
Viburnum x bodnantense 'Dawn', 66
  V. fragrans, 75
  V. plicatum 'Mareisii', 71
  V. tinus, 71
Vinca minor, 73
Vitis 'Black Hamburgh', 91
  V. 'Muscat of Alexandria', 91
Viola labradorica, 73

W

Weigela florida 'Variegata', 69
window, in yew hedge, 23